Debbie Slittman

DEAFNESS IN INFANCY
AND EARLY CHILDHOOD

MEDCOM PRESS CREDO

We believe

... that the communication of medicine should move as quickly as medicine itself.

... that new insights into the diagnosis and treatment of disease are too important to await the traditional delays of traditional medical book publishing.

... that communicating today's medicine, today, is the MEDCOM PRESS commitment to better health care delivery.

Robert E. Fuisz, M.D., *Publisher*

Virginia A. Malfitan, M.D., *Medical Director*

Robert B. Wilson, *Executive Editor*

DEAFNESS IN INFANCY AND EARLY CHILDHOOD

Editor

Peter J. Fine, MD

*Medical Director
Gallaudet College
Washington, D.C.*

Publishers
Robert E. Fuisz, MD
Richard C. Fuisz, MD

Director, Faculty of Medicine
George W. Thorn, MD

Chairman, Department of Medicine
David P. Lauler, MD

Director, Medical Affairs
Virginia A. Malfitan, MD

Vice President
Alfred R. Kelman

Executive Editor
Robert B. Wilson

Editorial Operations Manager
Peter Parks

Managing Editor, MEDCOM PRESS
Jane Lassner

Executive Art Director
Gary N. Olivo

Project Art Director
Tere LoPrete

Production Manager
Steve Montalbano

Production Director
George Nickford

MEDCOM®
World leader in multimedia medical education programs
2 Hammarskjöld Plaza New York, New York 10017 (212) 832-1400
Copyright©1974 by MEDCOM, Inc.
All rights reserved
Printed in the United States of America
No part of this publication may be reproduced, stored in a retrieval system or transmitted, in any form or by any means, electronic, mechanical, photocopying, recording or otherwise, without the prior written permission of the publisher.

MEDCOM MEDICAL UPDATE SERIES: SPECIAL PUBLICATION

Library of Congress CIP Data
Fine, Peter J
  Deafness in infancy and early childhood
  1. Children, Deaf. I. Title. [DNLM: 1. Deafness
—In infancy and childhood. WV270 F495d 1973]
RJ496.D4F56   362.7'8'42   73-17327
ISBN O-8463-0135-0
FIRST PRINTING

Contents

Contributors ix

Preface xiii
    Edward C. Merrill, Jr.

What's the Problem? And the Solution? 1
    An Interview with Peter J. Fine

Achieving Normalcy 9
    Taras B. Denis
A teacher of deaf children for over 20 years, Mr. Denis gives his views on the influence of parental attitudes ... the school environment ... and educational patterns used for deaf children.

PART I: PERSPECTIVES FROM A MEDICAL VIEWPOINT

Medical Aspects of Deafness 19
    Robert J. Ruben
In Dr. Ruben's thorough review of the physician's management of a deaf child, he discusses early diagnosis of deafness ... proper referrals ... the right kind of history ... and genetic information to be gleaned.

PART II: PSYCHOLOGICAL ASPECTS OF DEAFNESS

The Social and Psychological Development of the Deaf Child: Problems and Treatment...... 55
    Kenneth Z. Altshuler
Dr. Altshuler offers his extensive clinical experience in detailing the effects of deafness on the child ... on his family ... and on his psychological development.

Psychological Aspects in Diagnosing Deafness in a Child . 87
    McCay Vernon
A professor of psychology with much clinical experience, Dr. Vernon presents constructive ways of coping.

PART III: THE EDUCATION OF DEAF CHILDREN

Schools for Deaf Children 103
    David M. Denton, Richard G. Brill,
    Margaret S. Kent, and Nancy M. Swaiko
The history of educating deaf children and the goals of this education are discussed.

Total Communication as a Basis of Educating Deaf Children 132
    Richard G. Brill
Dr. Brill details his educational system of choice, Total Communication—designed to use all the communication possibilities left to the deaf child.

The Superior IQ's of Deaf Children of Deaf Parents 151
    Richard G. Brill
What do deaf parents do for their deaf children that hearing parents do not?

Two Children: A Study in Contrasts 162
    Lawrence Newman
Mr. Newman's account of raising his deaf daughter is illuminating and satisfying.

PART IV: SIGN LANGUAGE: ITS VARIATIONS AND ITS RELATIONS TO ENGLISH

ASL and Siglish: The Various Forms of Sign Language .. 189
    Louie J. Fant, Jr.
The richness of sign language is explored and its numerous varieties defined and discussed.

Ameslan: The Communication System of Choice 205
    Louie J. Fant, Jr.
Mr. Fant describes what for him is the near-perfect communication system for deaf people.

PART V: HEARING CHILDREN OF DEAF PARENTS

Effects of Parents' Deafness on Hearing Children 219
    McCay Vernon
Dr. Vernon presents data explaining how hearing children of deaf parents are often required to grow up before their peers.

Experiences of Two Hearing Children of Deaf Parents ... 225
    Louie J. Fant, Jr. and John S. Schuchman
Mr. Fant and Dr. Schuchman, both professionals in deafness and both hearing sons of deaf parents, offer their personal views of growing up in a deaf family.

Index 230
    Kieth C. Wright

Contributors

Kenneth Z. Altshuler, MD
Associate Clinical Professor of Psychiatry
Columbia University College of Physicians and Surgeons
Unit Chief, Rockland State Hospital
Psychiatric Services for the Deaf
New York, New York

Richard G. Brill, EdD
Superintendent, The California School for the Deaf
Riverside, California

Taras B. Denis, EdM
Guidance Counselor
The New York School for the Deaf
White Plains, New York

David M. Denton, PdD
Superintendent, The Maryland School for the Deaf
Frederick, Maryland

Louie J. Fant, Jr., MA
Lecturer in Special Education
California State University
Northridge, California

Peter J. Fine, MD
Assistant Clinical Professor of Pediatrics
and Otorhinolaryngology
Albert Einstein College of Medicine of Yeshiva University
Bronx, New York
Medical Director
Gallaudet College
Washington, DC

Margaret S. Kent, MA
Principal, The Maryland School for the Deaf
Frederick, Maryland

Edward C. Merrill, Jr., PhD
President, Gallaudet College
Washington, DC

Lawrence Newman, MA
Area Supervisor
Taft School
Program for the Aurally Handicapped
Santa Ana, California
President, International Association of Parents of the Deaf
Columnist, The Deaf American

Robert J. Ruben, MD
Professor of Otorhinolaryngology and
Department Chairman, Otorhinolaryngology
Albert Einstein College of Medicine of
Yeshiva University
Bronx, New York

John S. Schuchman, PhD, LLD
Dean of Students
Gallaudet College
Washington, DC

Nancy M. Swaiko, MA
Teacher, The Maryland School for the Deaf
Frederick, Maryland

McCay Vernon, PhD
Professor of Psychology
Western Maryland College
Westminster, Maryland
Editor, American Annals of the Deaf

Kieth C. Wright, PhD
Assistant Professor of Library Science
and Chief Librarian
Gallaudet College
Washington, DC

Preface

By treating illness and restoring patients to happier, more productive lives, today's medical practitioner makes a tremendous contribution to society. But there are times when a person's life can be saved only at the price of leaving him with a permanent handicap. This is the point at which rehabilitation procedures and special education programs step in by assisting an individual through a difficult adjustment period and helping him get into the mainstream of life once again.

This book is edited by a man who has been there. His life was saved by skillful surgery, but he will live out the rest as a deaf person. The trauma of this event has come and gone. He has accepted his deafness; he has developed skills to compensate for his hearing loss; he has adjusted his family life and returned to his profession as a practicing physician, seeing patients again on a daily basis.

Dr. Peter Fine has something to say to his medical colleagues which no other person can say as well. He wants them to know more about deafness and to become more sensitive to its psychological and social impact. He wants to share the difficulties of establishing dependable communication with family, friends, and colleagues, upon which one's humanity and intellectual being depend so heavily. Finally, Dr. Fine wants to enlist the continued interest and support of the medical profession in building a better world for those persons who suffer a severe hearing impairment. This is a very special book for those who sustain life and hope from day to day.

                                    Edward C. Merrill, Jr.
                                    President, Gallaudet College
                                    September, 1973

For Mary, without whom this book would
have been impossible,
and
for Taras, whose continual inspiration
served as its guideline

What's the Problem? And the Solution?
•
An Interview with PETER J. FINE

For centuries, deafness has generated controversy, conflict, curiosity, but above all, neglect. Doctors ignored deaf people; psychologists made few attempts to understand them; teachers simply threw up their hands at the thought of trying to educate a deaf child; and parents quietly despaired.

Dr. Peter Fine admits having once been merely curious about deafness, too—that is, until he lost his own hearing. Then his attitude turned about-face, and this book is one of the results of his changed attitude.

In this interview with MEDCOM, Dr. Fine emphasizes his views that proper understanding and treatment can put an end to neglect and help deaf children eventually participate in modern society as mature and healthy adults.

MEDCOM: How do most doctors react to deaf patients?

DR. FINE: To put it briefly, too many still dismiss deafness as little more than a curious disease or abnormality. I must admit that I felt this way myself before I became deaf. For instance, I can remember seeing only two deaf patients in my practice, and at that time I made no attempt to understand their communications, which were incomprehensible to me. They happened to be teen-aged sisters, and I relied on their understanding and helpful mother to interpret their symptoms so that I could treat them. I regarded their deafness as a mere curiosity that comes along only once in a blue moon, and I would guess that many doctors react the same way, viewing such a case as only another oddity in a long day's work. We really con't hold doctors solely responsible for such an attitude, though, because there are too few medical schools where treatment of deafness is part of the curriculum. As far as I know, no medical school in the country teaches the total management of deafness. Dr. Ruben has a great deal to say about this.

MEDCOM: But the two teen-aged girls came to you for treatment of a complaint that wasn't related to their deafness, didn't they? How should a doctor handle a patient whose main complaint is loss of hearing?

DR. FINE: To answer that question best, let's find out what happens when two anxious parents first bring their baby to a doctor or audiologist for consultation. The parents suspect deafness and are at the point where they want to know the truth, one way or another. Will their baby eventually hear, or will he always be deaf? They hope the examiner will say there's nothing to worry about; at the same time they fear that their suspicions will be confirmed.

The wise physician recognizes their conflict and does all he can to help them accept the fact of deafness. It won't do to give false reassurances—that is, to let these two parents continue to hope that their child will "outgrow" his disability. Instead, the doctor should be prepared to show them how to adapt to routines that will give their offspring a chance for a healthy, normal life. It's not so terribly difficult—just by emphasizing and going through plans for the medical, psychological, cultural, and educational well-being of their child, the doctor accomplishes a great deal. For example, many parents waste a great deal of time and money going from doctor to doctor in a vain effort to deny that deafness is the problem. Other parents may feel guilty for their child's handicap—consciously or unconsciously—and become bogged down in useless recriminations either against themselves, their mate, or even the child! The doctor who dispels these illusions at the outset helps to shorten this period of helpless floundering. This is not meant to imply that parents should not mourn for the loss of one of their child's most crucial senses. As physicians and others in the helping professions are becoming more aware of the psychological problems accompanying a handicap, so too must they learn to allow their patients to ventilate their feelings and guide them into constructive channels.

It's well to remember, too, that these two parents are not so helpless as they appear; otherwise they would not have taken the first step—to seek professional help. They come to you wanting to know, "Will our baby ever talk?" The doctor cannot answer that at the outset, of course, but he can point out that the sooner a two-way path of communication begins, the sooner their baby will take his rightful place within the family—as a lively, contributing member.

MEDCOM: You say that accepting deafness is the first step in rehabilitation. But won't many parents worry about their deaf child's feeling different from his peers? What else can they do to help give him a normal life?

DR. FINE: They'll worry, of course, and coping with a deaf child is no easy task. But fortunately, nearly all parents want their children to grow up healthy, don't they? The crucial difference between the needs of the hearing child and those of the deaf child is painstaking care and patience. The deaf child must not be made to feel different or alien, but he must neither be spoiled nor deprived. The aim must be for that middle ground where he can take his rightful place in the family. That is a sound and healthy psychological goal, quite attainable once the parents are able to meet their child's special needs.

MEDCOM: Acceptance, then, is the first hurdle. What comes after acceptance?

DR. FINE: Well, how to communicate is probably the most important thing to learn. Now, while there are many theories and systems of communication, perhaps the most effective one is called Total Communication, and I'll say more about that in a moment. What is paramount, however, is to get across the point that it matters very little which language system a parent uses, so long as two-way communication begins early—even in the cradle.

But to return to those two anxious parents, their next concern is how to communicate with their baby—a task that seems hopeless at first. The doctor can help by explaining a little about alternate forms of communication. Now this may sound easy, but the fact is that an age-old conflict rages between those who favor one system over another—between the "oral" or speech-reading school, and the "manual" school of sign language. The best course the doctor can follow is to side-step the conflict by placing the two systems into the concept of Total Communication. I don't mean to imply that all of these things can be used at the same time with an infant. Obviously, language acquisition is of primary importance, and I don't necessarily mean English or any other so-called formal language. I mean that the best way to get things across to an infant is to use "home-made" signs. Every author in this book stresses the same point; start simply and let the child lead himself.

MEDCOM: You just mentioned that Total Communication is perhaps the most effective system of communication. Can you tell why?

DR. FINE: Because Total Communication—simultaneous use of sign language, fingerspelling, electronic amplification of sound (hearing aids), the written word, and speech—removes the barriers which isolate a deaf child and his parents from each other at a very early age.

To the parent of a deaf baby, perhaps no moment is so poignant as the first time the joy of comprehension spreads between them. Needless to say, at that moment vast new frontiers open for everyone in the family. That is what we are after, and Total Communication seems to accomplish this best.

Studies show that deaf children who begin with speechreading and sign language in the cradle develop tremendously higher language and learning capacities and skills than those who do not. If a deaf toddler knows a sign language, he can absorb ideas and meanings as fast as his peers who acquire their language by ear. At the same time, the deaf child also develops the vital ability to abstract. Later on, when he is ready for school, he will have a great advantage over those children who know only one communication system. Some schools use both forms simultaneously in the beginning.

MEDCOM: Isn't it awfully hard to learn sign language? What do you say to parents who think they won't be able to master it?

DR. FINE: Of course, some parents may initially rebel at the thought of using sign language, but the truth is that sign language is quite easily learned and even more easily used once the basics are absorbed. Using the signs daily becomes second nature to anyone with minimum language skills. As a matter of fact, sign language can be used to express even the finest nuances in communication. Parents who learn it right from the beginning soon look upon its use as just another routine part of raising a child.

MEDCOM: What about speechreading?

DR. FINE: Communicating by speechreading really only presents a problem, since even the best, most skilled speechreader understands only 45 percent of spoken language. He has to piece together and guess at the missing 55 percent. The less skilled comprehend even less and, obviously, remain further in the dark. As Dr. Vernon points out, the best speechreaders are not deaf—they are hearing people. And 45 percent is an optimistic guess.

Fortunately, the relatively new concept of Total Communication has gone a long way toward obviating the conflict between the oral versus the manual proponents. I hope that many more educators of deaf children, and even deaf people themselves, can resolve further argument and agree that Total Communication is the system of choice.

MEDCOM: What about education? Are there special resources for the deaf child's social and cultural needs?

DR. FINE: Indeed there are, and often the burden of proper referral rests with the first person the parents see who confirms deafness as a diagnosis. He may not be a doctor, incidentally. Parents may consult an audiologist before they see a physician; if they do, they are more likely to receive needed information, simply because an audiologist works with deaf clients a great deal more than a physician does. In any case, both professionals should know where parents may turn for further help close to home, whether they are near a large metropolitan center or in a rural area.

The first source is the telephone book, which lists a number of agencies where parents can find proper information and guidance. In large cities, there are centers for deaf people. State and federal agencies also help. All are set up to guide parents toward acceptance and understanding.

Some parents worry about the cost of special education and training. To decide what realistic financial realignments will be necessary while still maintaining a healthy family balance, many agencies can help them come to a decision they can live with comfortably. For example, the Office of Vocational Rehabilitation has branches in each state. It is one of the main sources of financial aid for education and social life. The National Association of the Deaf, in Silver Springs, Maryland, near Washington, D. C., serves physicians, parents, and deaf children alike. The Council of American Instructors of the Deaf in Washington, D. C., gives helpful guidance and state schools for the deaf provide plentiful aid. Most are funded by state tax monies, charge little or nothing, and operate from the preschool years through high school with preparation for college.

To the resources just mentioned, I would also add this book, with the hope that readers will join those of us who are striving to make deafness a more normal way of life for those who do not hear. The contributors in this book represent many disciplines; some are doctors, some teachers, some psychologists. Some are deaf some are hearing. They write from differing points of view. Dr. Robert J. Ruben, for example, favors the development of a hospital-centered, total community for deaf children, while others feel the opposite is necessary. Regardless of our various points of view, however, all of us share the same ultimate goal: the healthy development of deaf infants and children.

In the world of education and communication, deaf children get too little too late. Here, Taras Denis explains why and suggests what can be done to give them more.

Achieving Normalcy
•
TARAS B. DENIS

The news that one's child is deaf is quite a shock to any parent. Unlike other, more visible handicaps, however, deafness may present problems which cannot simply be accepted and overcome, but which must be dealt with time and time again—unless parents understand the immediate need for their objectivity in rearing their child. As crucial as it is, love alone cannot help the deaf child develop into an independent, responsible adult.

From birth, the congenitally deaf child enters an unfair race in which obstacles have been set up under such terms as "normalcy," "education," and "communication"—the three problems dealt with here. Environment is an important factor in determining how these things are handled, as are time and place. For example, television can be helpful—but when is it "normal," when "educational," and when "communicative" for a deaf child? Normalcy itself is subject to change. Normalcy is flexible, after a fashion.

WHAT IS NORMALCY?

Even after deafness has been diagnosed, many parents try to hide the disability, from themselves as well as others. It is, after all, an invisible handicap, and one that tempts parents to keep the defect hidden—to serve their own frightened ends, to hide guilt, rejection, and, paradoxically, overprotection. This desire to shield deafness exists in many forms in the academic, vocational, and social world today. Parents who refuse to or cannot realistically face the problem, and who instead futilely seek "normalcy" at any price, risk years of educational inertia for their deaf child, as well as serious and often irreparable damage to his personality.

The child is deaf. Listening to music would be no more normal for him than racing would be for a crippled child. But there are other pleasures, other paths to happiness which the deaf child can pursue—all realistic and all within his reach.

A parent must not only recognize and accept the fact of the handicap but must let the deaf child determine his own need for assistance—just as normal-hearing children are allowed to do. Deaf children must develop their own independent values so that they, like everyone else, can grow to be independent people. The sooner this is realized—first by the doctor or audiologist who diagnoses and treats the child, then later by his teachers—the sooner the child can become a functioning, contributing individual. However, this process of development toward "normalcy" begins in the home, with the family—the environment that shapes the child's future, while he is still an infant.

WHAT DO WE MEAN BY EDUCATION?

Diversity of Opinions

Education as a concept conjures up many images. For some

people, a school, a classroom, or a teacher comes to mind. Others recall pupils sitting at their desks with hands folded or raised, heads bent in reading or writing, or friends running around the school yard during recess. This mood of childhood nostalgia best describes what are actually live, continuous, and uniquely human experiences that affect our adult lives.

All education is a dynamic process, constantly expanding and changing. Its crystallization into one concept is simply not possible. Even when a few ideas about education seem to jell, they too are in time removed, reevaluated, discarded, adjusted, or refrozen for later recall.

An education is so many things that to presuppose a single, rigid route toward its attainment is ridiculous, especially for a child with no hearing. It is a mistake to assume that all deaf children are similar in personality and intelligence. Nothing could be more naive. Except for his physical disability, the deaf child is as diverse, positively and negatively, as his hearing counterpart; and too frequently, it is the emphasis on the disability that blots out his individuality.

What Does a Deaf Child's Education Include?

One thing that education for the majority of deaf children does not include is the acquisition of normal speech or even written English comparable to that of hearing peers. Parents would be well advised to be wary of schools for deaf children that initially promise such achievements, for precious years may pass before nondelivery becomes apparent. They should be skeptical, too, of a doctor who handily offers his own personal prescription for the entire future development of a human being. The doctor's diagnosis may be scientifically correct, but his prescription for a "cure" may be unscientifically opinionated.

> //A deaf child's education must incorporate the realities of his soundless world, permitting him to develop his own distinct personality and life-style.//

An education for a deaf child should be one that is normal for him. It must incorporate the realities of his soundless world, permitting him to develop his own distinct personality and life-style. He must be allowed to learn all he can from the situations around him. He must be helped to realize his potential through information, ideas, and values useful to and selected by him. Such an education best serves the deaf child's needs from crib through Commencement Day.

Are Schools for Deaf Children All Alike?

The vast majority of parents endow the school for their deaf child with an all-knowing, infallible, and unimpeachable authority, partly because they want the school to be that way and partly because they are ignorant. Actually, schools for deaf children thrive on a variety of theories that are seldom challenged because, for one thing, the disability naturally discourages scrutiny and, as with most sheltered institutions, accounting to the public is difficult.

The main theories more or less contradict one another. A few have even languished for so long in benign neglect that in some places experimentation is tantamount to treason. Furthermore, the proponents of various teaching techniques expound their own methods at the expense of others, even those that have been proven more successful, sometimes only because these others do not fit their school's particular philosophy. Thus, in some schools only a certain type of education is given to a certain type of deaf child, and the rest can go elsewhere.

Should the parents willingly take their child elsewhere? Let's find out.

COMMUNICATION: MORE THAN A WORD

Joey, 4 years old, has normal hearing. He is sitting on the floor of the living room watching a television cartoon. In another part of the house his mother is busy. She need not look in at this specific hour because he is learning by himself in the best of all possible ways—while enjoying the situation. In fact, he can't help learning.

Walter is 5 and the deaf son of deaf parents. He is viewing the same cartoon as Joey across the street. Suddenly he jumps up and rushes out of the room, returning quickly with his mother. Making her sit, he communicates his puzzled feelings in a mixture of signs and pantomime: several dogs are chasing a "cat," but then, surprise! The "cat" starts running backward with its tail up. But so do the dogs! Walter wants to know why so many dogs are afraid of that one small black and white "cat." "That is no 'cat,'" says his mother in signs, and she begins to explain that the black and white animal (here she spells S-K-U-N-K on her fingers) is able to give off a bad smell (holding her nose and frowning) when its tail goes up like this (and she points upward). To be sure, Walter's mother is not able to explain everything her child asks about television programs, but the value of their two-way communication speaks for itself. Because Walter has someone who can answer him during the day, he is learning.

Susan, the congenitally deaf daughter of normal-hearing parents down the street, is sharing the same show with her mother who talks and talks and talks to Susan. The child's pre-primary teacher insists that talking is the only way their daughter will ever become "normal." Yet her parents notice that Susan does not understand television programs or most of what her mother and father say. In fact, seldom does anyone succeed in getting her attention. Occasionally, little Susan tries to make herself "heard" with gestures and other natural signs that she and her peers share in secret, but her parents will have none of that—they consider it alien, even abnormal. Thus, the girl's attempts to communicate are crushed on the spot, and she loses the chance to take the first step toward true learning or to establish herself as a person. All told, the most valuable, viable period of Susan's life is permitted to lapse into a void, the outcome of which no one can predict with certainty.

Why Walter Excels

Walter and Susan's experiences illustrate the two major methods of communication in use today in homes where a deaf child is the family's focal point: the manual method, a natural and expedient system of formal and informal signs, and the oral method, a system of speechreading that is as unreliable as it is taxing. The oral system prevails in the pre-primary phase of deaf children's education throughout this country.

However, recent surveys, along with examination of school records for deaf children, show that deaf children of deaf parents tend to excel. Walter's natural, developmental use of signs and gestures to get his message across seems to confirm this, especially when contrasted with Susan's frustration. An increasing number of psychologists, linguists,

> //Communication established at the crib level may explain why a deaf child of deaf parents excels.//

and childhood specialists are also beginning to recognize that communication established at the crib level may explain why a deaf child of deaf parents excels.

By ignoring these findings or by postponing for perhaps a year or two the vital need for early communication, hearing parents of a deaf infant impose an additional handicap right on top of the obvious one, thus depriving him of the chance to advance by whatever means possible.

Walter's preschool use of signs does not mean that he won't be just as facile one day with speech and speech-reading; the manual method does not obviate the oral. But his deaf parents wisely place his mental health and well-being first, and if the oral system helps him to achieve his full potential, so much the better.

What Early Signing Accomplishes

There is no mystery in Walter's family's method; it is simply developmental. The deaf family initiates communication straightaway with simple, basic gestures that the baby soon picks up and feeds back. Gradually, formal signs are introduced, and contrary to what pure oral educators think, rudimentary speech usually accompanies the gesture or sign. Thus in this reciprocal fashion, a deaf child's natural language ability is enhanced. Once in school, with a natural head start he can progress as far as his potential allows if the school's policy is relaxed.

There is no reason why hearing parents should not consider adopting the above developmental pattern. Signing is a beautiful experience, easy and fun to learn, especially when paced by a baby. Not only is parental interest repaid in kind but the possibilities for combining signs and speech are that much greater. The main thing to avoid is continuous, one-way communication; instead, give the child the chance to feed back with the rights and privileges of a unique individual. Unless two-way communication takes place, parents will continue talking to themselves and their deaf child will remain a robot whose controls are not in his hands.

As many of us begin to realize what our children have known all along—that theirs has been an education more for the sake of established norms than for themselves—shall we allow it to continue? If parents are to be parents, they must permit their children to be, simply, children—learning for themselves and no one else.

Part I:
DEAFNESS FROM A MEDICAL VIEWPOINT

Dr. Ruben describes the path physicians follow to diagnose the diseases associated with hearing loss, emphasizing that finding the cause determines the treatment.

Medical Aspects of Deafness
•
ROBERT J. RUBEN

INTRODUCTION

The deaf or hearing-impaired individual is a patient whose major symptom is his inability to hear properly. The hearing loss is only a symptom. This symptom, like any other, is an indication of a disease process. There are a multitude of disease processes that result in loss of hearing, and the patient whose major symptom is hearing loss may have a number of these other diseases. Too often physicians will call the symptom the disease and not recognize what the real disease is. A useful analogy would be to say that a patient with a high fever is suffering from the disease of fever and look no further. Such an operational definition would be disastrous, as the physician would not determine if the fever was caused by pneumonia, meningitis, appendicitis, etc. Unfortunately, many physicians look upon hearing loss as a disease and do not attempt to define which disease is causing the hearing loss.

The following paragraphs will approach the problem of hearing loss as that of a multitude of different diseases. The various etiological factors associated with deafness, the special aspects of these different diseases, the associated organ-system deficiencies, and the special relationship of deafness to general medical conditions will be discussed. This chapter will serve as a guide to the total medical management of individuals with a hearing loss.

ETIOLOGY

The first task that the physician has in the medical management of a patient with a hearing loss is to determine why his patient has the hearing loss. Audiometric studies usually enable the physician to determine what portion of the hearing mechanism is damaged. This allows the physician to begin to construct a reasonable differential diagnosis. The etiological factors of hearing loss are classified in three traditional groups: acquired, genetic, and unknown.

The most important aspect in arriving at the correct etiolgical factor is a careful history, including the possibility of consanguinity. A detailed genetic history is mandatory in most cases, especially with children. If the family history suggests genetic disease or if there is no positive history of acquired disease, audiometric studies should be obtained from immediate members of the family. Many times relatives who are not clinically deaf will have hearing losses which are detectable by audiometry. This information is useful in making a presumptive diagnosis of a recessive gene for deafness or a dominant gene with incomplete penetrance causing the deafness.

The family history should include not only queries about deafness but also specific questions concerning the more common genetic diseases that may present as part of the deafness syndrome, such as unilateral hearing loss; a white forelock; different-colored irides; kidney disease; blindness; thyroid dysfunction, especially goiter; brain tumor; etc.

The prenatal history of the patient must be carefully recorded. If the mother has taken any type of medication, this medication must be identified. The mother should be asked about any illnesses during her pregnancy. Both the mother and the child should be tested for rubella antibodies; a rubella antibody titer should be done at least in the mother if the child has already been immunized to rubella. The child should be tested for syphilis. At the present time the most reliable test is the Treponema pallidium immobilization test.

The possibility of attempted abortion by medication must always be considered. Many times quinine or one of the cytotoxic agents may have been used, and these drugs may result in deafness. It should be determined if other ototoxic drugs were used during pregnancy, especially the antitubercular drugs.

The perinatal history should be carefully reviewed with respect to prematurity, kernicterus, respiratory distress syndrome, ototoxic medication, birth trauma, meningitis, and anoxia. It is advisable to obtain a copy of the medical chart of the birth and neonatal care. This should include the nursing notes and the doctor's order sheets, so that the amount and type of medication which the neonate received can be ascertained.

A complete medical history of the young child must be obtained. Special emphasis should be placed on a possible history of meningitis, ototoxic medication, head trauma, and possible labyrinthitis.

The medical history of older children and adults should include all of the above. In addition, special emphasis must be placed upon ototoxic medication and sound trauma. Usually questions are asked about the more common ototoxic drugs, but two drugs which are often overlooked are aspirin and quinine. Aspirin ototoxicity will be found in patients with severe osteoarthritis. Quinine ototoxicity may occur in patients who are drug addicts, as quinine is commonly used to dilute some of the more commonly used narcotics.

The establishment of a correct etiological cause for the hearing loss allows the physician to offer a prognosis, begin to look for other associated problems, offer proper genetic counseling, and in some instances institute medical and/or surgical therapy. Without a proper diagnosis as to the etiology of deafness, medical care of the diseases of deafness cannot be carried out.

OTOLOGICAL CARE OF THE DEAF PATIENT

There are special otological considerations in the medical care of a deaf individual. One of the most important is the need for audiometric testing, as most deaf individuals usually have some hearing. A significant proportion of the diseases that can cause deafness are progressive. Continually assessing the hearing acuity will alert the physician to the possible need for any change in sound amplification for patients with hearing aids. The physician may need to institute other remedial factors such as lipreading. It is much easier to institute lipreading in a patient with a severe hearing loss than in a patient with a profound hearing loss.

Otitis Media

The problem of further hearing loss from serous or mucoid otitis media in a patient with a neurosensory hearing loss is one which too few clinicians recognize, although it is relatively simple to understand. A patient who has a hearing loss at 20 dB ISO will hear sound at 0.001 dynes/cm^2. If the patient has a serous otitis media, the hearing level may increase to 40 dB. The patient will then hear sound at 0.01 dynes/cm^2. The patient will need 0.009 dynes/cm^2 more sound energy to hear, not a large increase in sound pressure for the patient to be able to hear.

If a patient has a neurosensory loss so that he normally hears at 80 dB, he will need 1.0 dynes/cm^2 to hear. This patient with the neurosensory hearing loss acquires a serous otitis media and his hearing level is reduced the same amount as the normal patient, i.e., 20 dB to 100 dB. The sound energy needed at 100 dB is 10 dynes/cm^2. The patient with the neurosensory hearing loss will need an additional 9 dynes/cm^2 to hear, a very large increase in sound energy.

The patient with the neurosensory hearing loss and serous otitis media will need 1000 times the amount of sound energy to hear than the patient with normal hearing loss and serous otitis media (0.009 dynes/cm^2 × 1000 = 9 dynes/cm^2). It is obvious that the same disease process, serous otitis media, will cause a much greater hearing deficit in the patient with a neurosensory hearing loss than in a normal patient.

Diagnosis of a serous otitis media patient with severe to profound hearing loss cannot be done with conventional audiometry, because the thresholds needed to detect bone conduction are equal to or greater than the tactile thresholds and/or the limits of most conventional bone oscillators. The diagnosis of serous otitis media, or other conductive components, in the patient with severe to profound neurosensory hearing loss will depend upon the physical examination of the external auditory meatus and tympanic membrane, impedance audiometry, and tympanometry.

Examination of the external auditory canal may reveal a simple problem, such as impacted cerumen or an otitis externa. Ocassionally the canal may be closed by an osteoma or some other tumor.

Examination of the tympanic membrane is very important in making a diagnosis of serous otitis media in the patient with a neurosensory hearing loss. The clinician must first have an accurate picture of the appearance of a normal tympanic membrane. Unfortunately, most modern texts and contemporary teaching give only a superficial view of the

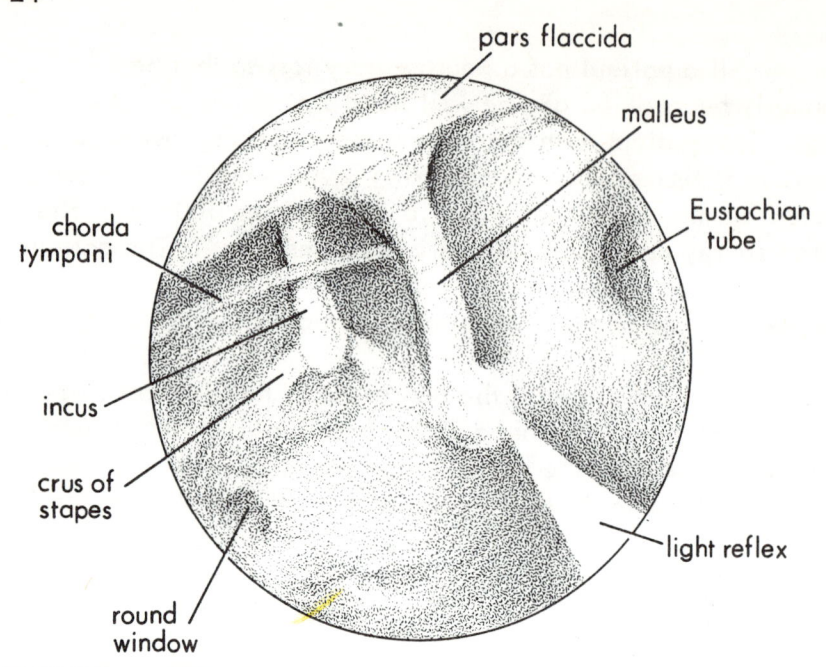

FIGURE 1 Diagram of tympanic membrane illustrating the landmarks which should be seen through a normal translucent tympanic membrane.

tympanic membrane. The normal tympanic membrane (Fig 1) is a thin, transparent-to-translucent membrane. The clinician, with adequate lighting, should be able to see the malleus, the long process of the incus, part of the cura of the stapes, the light reflex and many times the corda tympani, stapedius tendon, shadow of the eustachian tube orifice, and shadow of the round window niche. The tympanic membrane should be straight with no inflammation and very little vascularity. As an individual ages, there will be changes in the tympanic membrane due to infections. These

//Most adult tympanic membranes will be not normal but average.//

changes include calcium deposits in the drum and thickening of the drum with opacity and scarring. Most adult tympanic membranes will be not normal but average because of these changes. However, if the drum is just average or shows signs of active disease—eg, retraction, bulging, air-fluid levels, perforation, etc.,—the clinician must suspect a possible conductive hearing loss.

The physical examination, especially in infants and children, will not completely determine if the individual with a severe to profound neurosensory hearing loss has a conductive component associated with the hearing loss. Another independent index of middle ear disease must be used. The second method of ascertaining the function of the middle ear in a patient with severe to profound neurosensory hearing loss is impedance audiometry and tympanometry (Fig 2).

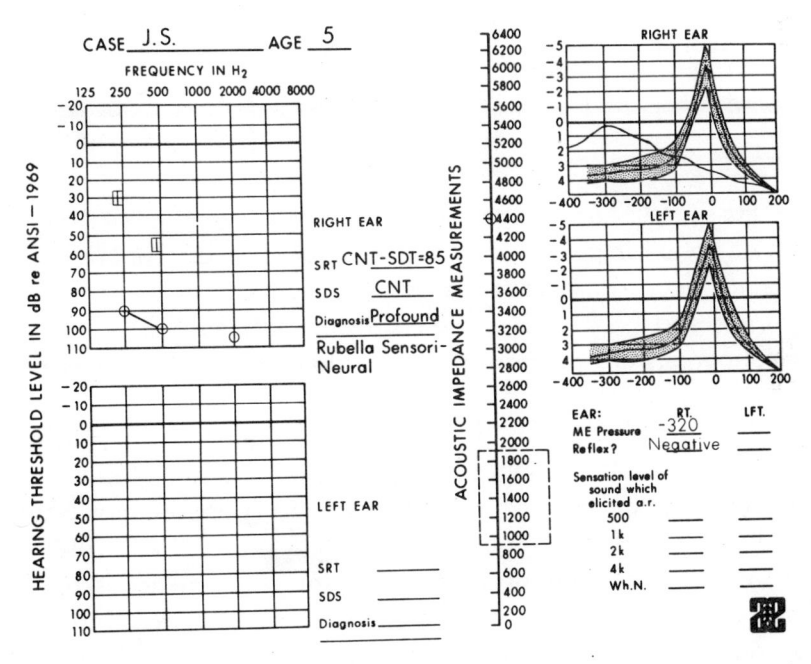

FIGURE 2 In A & B, similar audiometric findings of possible bone air gap in children with profound neurosensory hearing loss. (A) JS, age 5, appears to have a bone air gap at 250 and 500 cycles per second. The intensity needed to elicit the response is in the tactile range. A conductive component can be surmised from the high impedance of 4400 acoustic ohms, the abnormal tympanogram with the shift to the left, and the negative ear pressure of -320 mm of water.

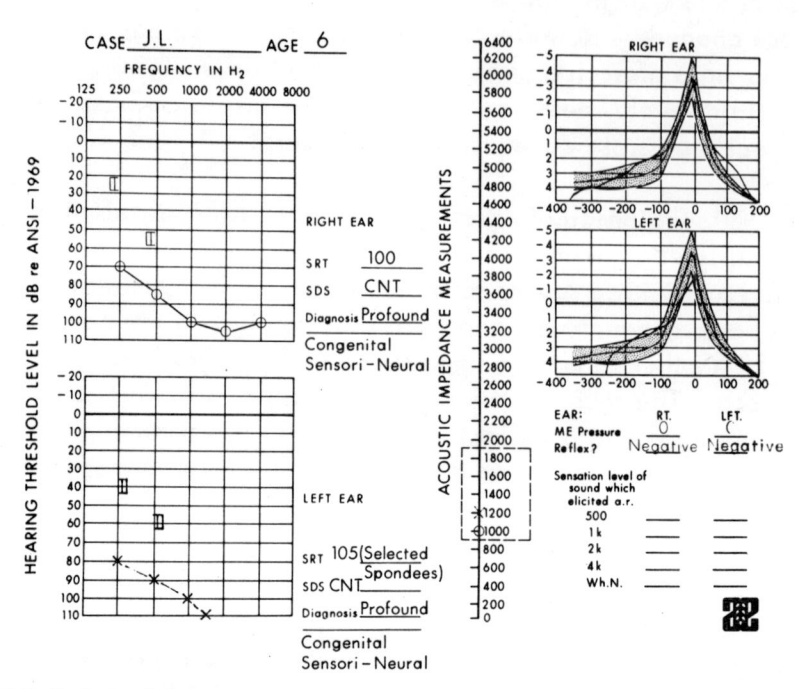

FIGURE 2 (B) Another patient, JL, age 6, with a similar type of bone air gap in the tactile range. These ears reveal a normal acoustic impedance of 1000 acoustic ohms in the right ear and 1200 acoustic ohms in the left ear. The tympanograms are normal and the middle ear pressure is normal.

Impedance audiometry and tympanometry can tell the clinician the relative acoustic impedance of the middle ear, the middle ear pressure, the form of movement of the tympanic membrane, and the status of the stapedius reflex. A patient with serous otitis media will have an increase in the relative acoustic ohms, a marked decrease in middle ear pressure, restricted movement of the tympanic membrane, and absence of the stapedius reflex. The presence of any or all of these findings will indicate abnormal function of the middle ear, very highly correlated with a conductive hearing loss.

A careful examination of the external auditory canal and tympanic membrane with impedance audiometry and tympanometry will allow the clinician to diagnose conductive components in patients with severe to profound neurosensory hearing loss. ==The most common pathology encountered, especially in infants and children, is serous or mucoid otitis media.== The treatment is simple and direct. The patient should be examined to determine if there is any anatomical disease causing the condition. The most common findings are malformation of the palate (cleft palate, submucosal cleft of the palate, etc.), midfacial malformations (Crouzon's disease, Alport's disease, etc.), or a nasopharyngeal mass (hypertrophy of adenoids, choanal polyps, tumors of the nasopharynx, etc.). The presence of systemic diseases such as allergy, blood dyscrasia, hypoimmunity, bone diseases (otosclerosis, Paget's disease, osteogenesis imperfecta, osteoporosis, etc.) must also be considered. After a correct diagnosis is made of the middle ear problem, treatment should be started.

The most common form of therapy, especially in children, is to insert middle ear ventilating tubes for serous otitis media. Middle ear ventilating tubes do not interfere with the wearing of hearing aids. The aid can be replaced on the ear approximately two or three days after the middle ear ventilating tube is inserted.

The problem of acquired and/or progressive middle ear hearing losses in patients with neurosensory hearing loss must be continually monitored by the clinician. Ideally, all patients with neurosensory hearing loss should be initially assessed with impedance audiometry and tympanometry. The patient should then have routine follow-up examinations. The schedule varies for different age groups. Infants and young children up to age 5 or 6 should have impedance audiometry and tympanometry performed two or three times a year, older children about twice a year, and adults once a year.

Otitis Externa

The patient who wears a hearing aid has a greater

risk of developing otitis externa than the population at large. The clinician must ascertain the cause of the otitis externa before he can properly treat the patient. The most common causes of otitis externa in patients wearing hearing aids are: (1) abrasion of the external auditory canal from an improperly fitted hearing aid mold; (2) infection of the external auditory canal from a dirty hearing aid; (3) allergy to the hearing aid; and (4) acquired infections from environmental sources such as a dirty swimming pool or careless cleaning of the ear.

The first possible cause, an improperly fitted hearing aid, is one of the more common and easiest to treat. The initial therapy should consist of cleaning the external auditory canal, using appropriate antibiotic medication, and after the infection is cured, obtaining a properly fitted mold. The size and shape of the auditory canal continually changes throughout life. The changes are most rapid in the infant and young child. New molds may have to be made in an infant or a young child twice a year until age 6 or 7. Adults may also have changes in their ear canals, and the mold must either be changed or tailored to fit the canal. Occasionally the skin of the external auditory canal may be very friable and sensitive to pressure of a hard but well-fitting mold. If this is the case, a new mold should be made of a softer substance.

The second problem, infection from a dirty ear mold, is treated first by controlling the initial infection and then by instructing either the parent or the patient how to keep the mold clean. A common problem contributing to a dirty mold and otitis externa is impacted cerumen. Hearing aid wearers should have their ears checked at least twice a year for cerumen. If there is impacted cerumen, this must be gently removed.

The third cause of otitis externa, an allergy to the material from which the hearing aid is made or to the solutions used to clean it, can be the most painful and difficult to care for. The initial treatment is to remove the mold and treat the otitis externa. A new mold must then be made from a material to which the patient is not allergic. There are hypoallergic substances available for such hearing aid molds. When the allergy is caused by the solution used to clean the mold, the cleaning solution should be changed and the mold carefully washed out after cleaning.

The last possible cause of otitis externa, from environmental causes, is treated by removing the hearing aid while the patient is being treated for the infection. The mold should be carefully cleaned so that it does not reinfect the ear when it is reinserted after the infection has been cured.

Cerebellopontile Angle Tumors

A cerebellopontile angle tumor is a rare but life-threatening disease which must be considered in all patients with neurosensory hearing loss. Too often, a physician sees a patient with a severe to profound neurosensory hearing loss and assumes that the entire problem is within the inner ear. All new patients with severe neurosensory hearing loss should be considered as possibly having a cerebellopontile angle tumor. Many times the history will preclude such a diagnosis, as with sudden loss of hearing after an explosion, after ototoxic medication, etc. However, more often than not the medical history of the hearing loss will not be that precise. The clinician should obtain further audiologic studies which include speech discrimination, tone decay, and recruitment tests, as well as a test of the vestibular function. If these tests reveal the possibility of retrocochlear pathology, x-ray studies of the internal auditory meati should be done. Usually the Stenver's and Towne's projections are the most suitable for seeing the internal auditory meatus. All patients, including children with unilateral neurosensory hearing loss, should have a complete audiological battery, if sufficient hearing remains; vestibular studies and x-rays of the internal auditory meatus are necessary so a cerebellopontile angle tumor can be ruled out.

Only Hearing Ear

Another special otological problem in the medical management of the deaf patient is that of an only hearing ear. Many times a patient will be totally deaf in one ear while the other ear has a moderate or severe hearing loss. This hearing ear must be protected, as it is the patient's only means for audition. The ear must be protected from, among other things, sound trauma.

The most common dilemma arising in caring for only one hearing ear is the advisability of some form of surgical treatment. An only hearing ear with recurrent fluid should be considered for the possible placement of a middle ear ventilating tube. This procedure involves relatively low risk to the inner ear and should be done when it is felt that the fluid in the ear may lead to labyrinthitis, mastoid disease, and/or cholesteatoma.

Chronic mastoid disease in an only hearing ear should be treated medically unless there are definite signs of approaching labyrinthine involvement; then surgery may be performed, with special care being taken not to open the labyrinth. This same advice applies to tympanic membrane perforations and cholesteatomas.

Surgery in an only hearing ear for reconstruction of middle ear function—eg, tympanoplasty, stapedectomy—is absolutely contraindicated. The risks of damaging the labyrinth are too great. If the hearing is lost, the patient becomes totally deaf. The hearing loss secondary to the conductive component can be treated quite well with a proper hearing aid with less risk to the patient's hearing.

MEDICAL INVESTIGATION OF PATIENTS WITH NEUROSENSORY HEARING LOSS

This section will be limited to the medical workup of neurosensory deafness, as the problems of the care and treatment of diseases of the external and middle ear are beyond the scope of this text. The reader is referred to any of the contemporary texts on otorhinolaryngology.*

The purpose of the medical investigation of a patient with neurosensory deafness is two-fold. The first is to find out if there is a treatable cause of the deafness and the second is to determine if the deafness is a symptom of a systemic disease. The otologist caring for a patient with neurosensory deafness must become, in the broad sense, a general physician.

The History

The initial history should ascertain the time at which the symptoms were first noted. There are significant differences in the types of neurosensory hearing loss between those in which the onset is gradual and those in which it is sudden. An example of this would be an adult who has noted a gradual neurosensory hearing loss in one ear, with increased difficulty in understanding speech. This history would indicate the strong possibility of a cerebellopontile angle tumor. Another example is a patient who notes a sudden hearing loss after doing his morning exercises. This could indicate the possibility of a traumatic perilymphatic fistula. The latter condition is thought to be potentially remediable.

There are five important associated symptoms with neurosensory hearing loss: vertigo, ear pain (otalgia), tinnitus,

*Paparella, Shumrick, Shambaugh, Ballantyne, Frazier, etc.

ear discharge (otorrhea), and a facial nerve abnormality.

Eliciting a history of vertigo as a symptom is sometimes quite difficult. The physician first needs a clear definition of what is generally meant by vertigo. This is most commonly defined as a sensation of either the patient or the environment revolving in space. It is important to emphasize the actual sensation of rotation and not to confuse vertigo with dizziness, which usually means the feeling of unsteadiness but not necessarily rotation. It is preferable to limit the definition of vertigo to a true rotary sensation, while all other feelings of movement would be described as dizziness. The clinical significance of differentiating between vertigo and dizziness is that most diseases of the vestibular labyrinth will be associated with vertigo and not with dizziness. On the other hand, systemic diseases such as hypertension, hypoglycemia, etc. will be associated with dizziness and not with vertigo as defined above.

Ear pain may be due to some infection, foreign body, or growth in the ear. Ear pain may also be a referred pain coming from a distant place, e.g., a tumor in the tonsillar fossa or the pharynx. Finding otalgia in the patient's history makes a physical examination mandatory to account for it. Ear pain is a relatively rare symptom with inner ear or VIIIth nerve disease.

Tinnitus as a symptom is important in helping determine which ear is affected. This is true if the tinnitus is heard in one ear or the other. When the sensation of noise or sound is heard in the middle of the head, or if it is not necessarily directed toward one side or the other, the physician looks for causes other than ear disease as responsible for the tinnitus. An important question to answer is, when does the tinnitus appear? A patient with a neurosensory hearing loss which is caused by sound trauma will usually state that there is tinnitus after exposure to loud noises, e.g., subway trains, gun shots, jet engine noise, a day in the factory, etc.

The type of sound perception which the patient has should be determined. Most cases of tinnitus associated with neurosensory hearing loss will be of the nature of buzzing or pure tones. Many times the audiologist can match a patient's tinnitus with one of the pure-tone frequencies generated by the audiometer. Throbbing or pulsating tinnitus may be associated with a vascular anomaly, e.g., a glomus tumor or aneurysm. All patients who have the symptom of tinnitus should be examined with a stethoscope for objective tinnitus to rule out the possibility of vascular disease.

The fourth important symptom is that of otorrhea. This is seldom encountered in neurosensory hearing loss. When the symptom is noted it may indicate either external or middle ear infection, and the cause of the discharge must be determined. The history of aural discharge must also be considered with a person wearing a hearing aid. If there is a chronic infection of either the external or middle ear, fitting a hearing aid with a mold must be deferred until the infection is cured. If the condition cannot be readily cured, as in a patient with an only hearing ear with chronic mastoid disease, a different type of hearing aid without a canal mold must be used.

It is imperative to pay careful attention to symptoms which can be associated with the facial nerve in the history of a patient with neurosensory hearing loss. The patient should be asked if there is any paralysis or weakness of the face muscles. If so, the time of onset of these symptoms should be noted. A history of congenital facial paresis or paralysis and a neurosensory loss would suggest a congenital lesion. Gradual facial paralysis or paresis with an associated neurosensory hearing loss would suggest a progressive lesion along the course of the facial nerve. This could be a tumor in the internal auditory meatus or in the middle ear. The affected portion of the facial nerve can be further defined by asking specific questions concerning the three branches of the facial nerve. The greater superficial petrosal nerve, located at the gasserian ganglion at the most proximal end of the internal auditory meatus, is the first branch.

Loss of function of the greater superficial petrosal nerve will cause a decrease in tearing in the ipsilateral eye. If the patient states that he has weakness of the face and a dry eye, there may be a lesion of the nerve proximal to the gasserian ganglion. The next branch of the facial nerve is the motor branch to the stapedius muscle. Loss of this branch of the facial nerve will occasionally elicit the symptom of hyperacousia, i.e., sound seeming louder in the affected ear. This symptom may also be due to recruitment in the affected ear. The third branch to be considered is the chorda tympani which supplies the afferent innervation of the anterior two thirds of the tongue predominantly for salt and sweet. The patient should be asked if he has noticed any change in taste or dryness of the mouth.

History of Young Children

Usually obtained from the parents, the history of an infant or young child with a neurosensory deafness should be so structured that information may be gained concerning the etiology of the neurosensory hearing loss. It is best to take a complete initial history and on subsequent visits to repeat the genetic history again. One should ask the parents to talk to the rest of the family to determine if there are any other relatives with hearing loss.

//Many times the parents may be second or third cousins and not realize it.//

The pediatric history will begin with an inquiry into the possibility of consanguinity between the parents. Many times the parents may be second or third cousins and not realize it. This information can be ascertained by asking the parents where the grandparents and great-grandparents were born.

The next step in the history is to construct a family tree. This is done in our clinics by writing down a classical family tree starting with the propositus. Each sibling is put on the family tree. Following this, the parents are placed and identified, as well as all of the parents' sisters, brothers, and their children. This is continued for the grandparents, the granduncles, grandaunts, the great-grandparents, etc. An attempt should be made to list the children of all relatives. The family tree is initially constructed at the first clinic visit and on subsequent clinic visits the family tree is reviewed. Many times on initial visits the parents will not know or remember the problems of their relatives. Only after several visits, when they have had time to discuss the problem with the family, will they be able to supply more information useful in determining the family pattern of hearing loss.

==Specific questions are posed concerning the hearing ability of each relative. If there is a hearing loss, the etiology of the loss should be determined.== It is important, especially for people born before 1900, to determine if the hearing loss was due to infection or was inherited. Mental retardation was often confused with deafness, especially if it occurred at the end of the 19th or the beginning of the 20th century. Information concerning mental retardation should be obtained. It is also important to inquire about other signs and symptoms of the more common genetic diseases.

The next part of the history is the prenatal history, including any instance of sickness (especially viral infections such as rubella), a history of increased Rh titer, attempted abortion, maternal use of potentially ototoxic antibiotics, and a history of maternal syphilis. The perinatal history should include a description of the course and duration of the labor, traumatic delivery, maternal infection, prematurity, perinatal infection (especially meningitis), anemia, and the use of any ototoxic medication.

The remainder of the history for infants and young children should elicit factors concerning subsequent infections, especially meningitis, ototoxic medication, and head trauma. It is also important to record the developmental landmarks, e.g., the ages of turning over, walking, and toilet training.

The parents must be asked if they think the child hears now or has heard in the past. Many times a very good history of a possible progressive hearing loss may be obtained. It is important to note whether the parents feel that the child has a fluctuating hearing loss. If this is so, the physician must consider the presence of middle ear fluids as a contributing factor.

History of the Adult

The history of an adult patient is taken in a similar manner, with less emphasis on the pre- and perinatal history

//The genetic history in an adult with neurosensory hearing loss is as important as in an infant.//

if the hearing loss has been acquired later in life. However, the genetic history in an adult with neurosensory hearing loss is as important as in an infant. Many patients will have a late-onset, progressive, neurosensory hearing loss which might be either an autosomal dominant or recessive. Special attention is given to the problem of noise trauma and ototoxicity in adults. The symptoms associated with neurosensory hearing loss caused by sound trauma are a neurosensory hearing loss with or without tinnitus that is exacerbated after exposure to loud noises. The hearing becomes better after a period of time, usually a matter of hours. Some patients seem to be unusually susceptible to loud noises. This clinically appears to happen most frequently in those patients who have an inherited neurosensory hearing loss. An example is a young man who had a ringing in his ears after attending maneuvers in an army reserve unit. He was an officer in an artillery unit and was subjected to a week or so of cannon firing. It was discovered that he had a moderate neurosensory hearing loss, and from his history it was noted that there were other people in his family with neurosensory hearing loss, who were found and tested. The patient exhibited a rather straightforward dominant with relatively homogeneous penetrance late-onset hearing loss. This patient's work required him to be exposed to loud noises, but his sensitivity was greater than most people's without this hearing loss. Upon recognition of his problem, ear defenders were prescribed, and he has been able to pursue his elected profession.

The physical examination of a patient with a neurosensory hearing loss is the same as for any patient seen by the otorhinolaryngologist. Special emphasis is placed on the neurological examination of the cranial nerves. All children with neurosensory hearing loss should have a careful examination of the eyes, including a funduscopic examination. This funduscopic examination should be repeated until age 20, as the problem of Usher's syndrome is important. Usher's syndrome is an autosomal recessive hearing loss associated with retinitis pigmentosa. Children initially suffer a hearing loss and later on develop decreased visual acuity. The funduscopic examination is also important in diagnosing congenital rubella by retinal changes and cataracts.

Examination of the ear should determine any anomalies in the pinna, external canal, and the tympanic membrane. Examination of the face should note any facial asymmetry or minor malformations. Examination of the mouth must note any palatal deformities, i.e., cleft palate, high arch palate, submucosal cleft of the palate, or bifid uvula. The velopharyngeal distance and function of the velopharyngeal musculature should also be made. Any of these conditions can contribute to a chronic serous otitis media which would further exacerbate a neurosensory hearing loss.

An examination of the nasopharynx must be done in every patient, preferably with a nasopharyngoscope. The eustachian tube orifices should be observed and any obstruction or dysfunction noted. An examination of the larynx, with a mirror, should be performed. The physician will be looking for both anatomical and physiological abnormalities of the pharynx and larynx. The neck examination should include palpation of both carotid arteries and the thyroid gland. There are a number of syndromes associated with thyroid abnormalities, one being Pendred's syndrome, associated with goiter.

The physical examination of the eye should also note a diversity of color, or heterochromia. Many times a person with Waardenburg's disease will have a difference of color in portions of the same iris. The hair should also be examined to see if there are any abnormalities in hair pigmentation.

It is very useful to take color photographs of a patient with neurosensory hearing loss to be reviewed later. Many times a genetic syndrome will be recognized upon subsequent review. Also, with the rapid identification of more genetic syndromes throughout the world, it would be wise to have a visible record of the patient. As these syndromes are described, patients can be matched with these syndromes.

Laboratory Studies

Fundamental laboratory studies are needed for the proper workup of a patient with a neurosensory hearing loss. These laboratory studies are designed to gain information about the extent and location of the hearing problem. They are also constructed in such a way to discover any underlying diseases of which the neurosensory hearing loss may only be a symptom. Laboratory studies should first include a hearing test or impedance audiometry. In cases of suspected genetic hearing loss, or when the etiology is unknown, it is important to assess the hearing acuity of as many members of the family as possible, including siblings, parents, aunts, uncles, and first cousins. Many times a diagnosis of genetic hearing loss can be made through relatives who have no clinical hearing loss but who have very definite and repeated audiological abnormalities. All patients with neurosensory hearing loss should undergo an electronystagmographic analysis of vestibular function. Two types of problems can be uncovered. The first type is in infants and young children who may have absent or markedly decreased vestibular function, thought possibly to result in temporary motor retardation. The second type is that patients with a gradual neurosensory hearing loss and absent or decreased function have a higher probability of having a mass in their internal auditory meatus than those patients with normal vestibular function.

Mastoid x-rays are obtained in all patients with neurosensory hearing loss. If the bony labyrinth is abnormal, there is a reasonable possibility that the patient also has an associated central nervous system malformation. The internal auditory meati are always examined to determine the probability of an internal auditory meatal tumor. A number of patients will also have x-ray findings which are compatible with chronic mastoid disease.

Rubella antibody titers of both the mother and child are obtained or, if the child has been immunized, of just the mother. Many times there are subclinical rubella infections during pregnancy which may result in the child's deafness. It is important to determine the etiology of deafness for the total management of the child. If the child has congenital rubella, the prognosis is liable to be somewhat more guarded, and more extensive testing of other affected systems, such as the eyes, heart, and central nervous system, will be done.

//All patients should have a test for either congenital or acquired syphilis.//

All patients, both children and adults, should have a test for either congenital or acquired syphilis. At the present time the Treponema pallidium immobilization test appears to be the best.

The patient is screened for renal disease by obtaining a blood urea nitrogen and/or serum creatinine and a complete urinalysis. There are a large number of genetic syndromes associated with renal deficiency. The most common appears to be Alport's disease, transmitted as an autosomal dominant with increased penetrance in the male. A patient with Alport's disease typically presents as a prepubescent boy with progressive neurosensory hearing loss. The urinalysis will reveal proteinuria, and the blood urea nitrogen may be increased. This is just one of a number of renal diseases associated with hearing loss. Congenital malformations of the pinna and/or middle ear are associated with gross renal malformations, e.g., horseshoe kidney, pelvic kidney, etc. Every child born with a malformation of the pinna and/or the external auditory canal should have an intravenous pyelogram to determine whether or not this associated renal abnormality is present. The abnormality is found in about 10% of patients with pinnal and/or external auditory canal malformations.

Blood studies are also obtained and should include a hematocrit, red blood cell count, differential and sedimentation rate. There are several hemoglobinopathies associated with neurosensory hearing loss; for example, Waldenstrom's macroglobulinemia can result in neurosensory hearing loss. Neurosensory hearing loss is also seen in leukemic patients and sometimes with serum protein abnormalities. A total serum protein and albumen/globulin ratio are also obtained.

An electrocardiogram is obtained in all children with neurosensory hearing loss, as there are a large number of associated, acquired, and genetic cardiac lesions. These include the cardiopathy of congenital rubella, the conduction defects noted in the Jervell-Lange-Nielsen syndrome, and others.

Each child with a neurosensory hearing loss must have a psychometric evaluation and speech and language evaluation. The results of these studies should only be considered as tentative. After a child has been diagnosed and put in a proper habilitative setting, there will probably be a significant increase in the child's performance in these areas.

The medical assessment of a child with a neurosensory hearing loss must be thorough. It is the patient's right and the physician's responsibility to obtain as much information as possible about the patient's disease. Only after this is done can appropriate therapy and habilitative programs be proposed.

GENETICS AND DEAFNESS

The etiology of deafness is usually divided into three groups: acquired, genetic, and unknown. In children, about 40% of deafness is acquired, 20% is genetic, and 40% is unknown. The relative frequency is probably similar for the adult population. The correct determination of the etiology of deafness is one of the most important aspects in the medical management of the patient. By determining the correct etiology, other associated conditions can be determined. A prognosis concerning further hearing loss may be made; proper treatment in those few areas which are treatable can be carried out, and genetic counseling may be done.

Clinical data concerning the etiology of deafness reveals that even with a very careful workup, about 40% of cases cannot be assigned to a known, acquired or genetic cause. When geneticists examine the deaf population, they manage to account for all cases. They call the unknown group recessive on theoretical grounds and call the mode of genetic transmission autosomal recessive. Their assignment of the group to autosomal recessive is based on several hypotheses.

The first hypothesis is that there are a large number of autosomal recessive genes for deafness in the population. Thus, each individual in the population has a high probability of carrying one recessive gene for deafness. Individuals carrying the recessive genes usually do not present with any overt symptoms of noticeable hearing loss and are superficially considered to be phenotypically normal.

The second hypothesis is that there are only a finite number of recessive genes. There is the possibility that two people carrying the same autosomal recessive gene will marry. Both of these people will be phenotypically normal. However, if they marry, one quarter of their children will be deaf. A child from this type of marriage would be worked up and placed in the unknown category. The geneticist's assumption is that this child can be considered on a probability basis as having recessive genetic disease.

Probability of Future Deaf Children

The parents of a deaf child will usually want to know whether or not they will have other deaf children. The advice is straightforward for a child who has had congenital rubella, meningitis, or any other definite acquired causes for deafness: The parents can be told that the probability of having another deaf child is the same as for the population at large, somewhat less than one in a thousand. The parents of a child with a known genetic syndrome can also be advised as to the probability of their having another deaf child. If the disease is autosomal dominant and only one parent is affected, then 50% of their children will be affected. Infrequently, both parents will have the dominant gene and all of their children will be affected. When the disease is autosomal recessive and each parent is heterozygous for the gene, one quarter of the children will be affected. If one parent is heterozygous and the other is homozygous, one half of their children will be affected. If both parents are homozygous for the same gene, which occasionally happens, then all their children will be affected. The last two situations are usually encountered in families which are inbred or in families which come from small religious and/or ethnic groups. It is also encountered in marriages between two deaf people. Sex-linked inheritance of deafness is rare but does occur.

//Genetic counseling must also be given to the parents of a child with deafness of unknown etiology.//

Genetic counseling must also be given to the parents of a child with deafness of unknown etiology. There are three possibilities: that the child has an unknown acquired deafness, that the child has a spontaneous mutation, or that both parents are heterozygotes for the same recessive deafness gene. The physician must attempt to ascertain whether or not the parents are gene carriers. This is done by carefully going over the family history. The clinician will attempt to determine if there is any deafness, any other syndrome associated with deafness, or any possibility of consanguinity. Occasionally the possibility of consanguinity may be found by determining the town or district from which the ancestors emigrated to America. A second method of determining if the parents are heterozygotes for a deafness gene is to obtain an audiological test of the parents. This should include air and bone conduction, speech discrimination, and a measurement of the threshold of the stapedius reflex. Quite frequently the parents will have similar types of hearing losses not clinically apparent but quite evident when they undergo audiological testing. The audiological testing is really a much more accurate determination of the parents' phenotype.

Even with the additional genetic history and audiometric examination of the parents, there will be a large number of cases in which there is no conclusive evidence of genetic disease. The parents of these children will want to know whether or not they will have any more deaf children. There have been a number of cases in our experience where the parents of a deaf child for which no etiology could be found have had other deaf children. All of these parents either have been given no genetic counseling or have been told that they would not have another deaf child. These experiences and the theoretical considerations of geneticists outlined in previous paragraphs indicate that genetic counseling is necessary for parents of the idiopathically deaf child. The parents are told that there is no known cause for the deafness in their child. However, because of the large number of recessive gene carriers and the finite number of recessive genes, they may indeed be carriers. Thus, they have an increased probability over the general population of having another deaf child. A precise probability statement cannot be given. The percentage is greater than one in one thousand births and may be as high as one in four. These parents must be informed that they are in a high-risk group for having other deaf children. The decision to have more children or not is their own personal, moral, ethical, and psychological problem. They must be honestly informed so they will have an accurate basis of information upon which to make their decision.

Genetic counseling also occurs frequently in adults with a hearing loss. The most common problem is the adult with a progressive hearing loss that has begun in his twenties or thirties. It has been found that these losses are transmitted either as a recessive or dominant trait. Most often the genetics of the family can be well worked out. The question of what effect the gene will have on their children occurs especially in dominant transmission. This is a very difficult question to answer in the dominantly transmitted, late-onset, progressive sensorineural hearing loss, because of the great amount of variability in the gene's expressivity. The physician must determine the amount of hearing loss in as many members of the family as possible. This information can then be shown to the couple so that they can see the effect of the gene in a large number of people similarly affected.

Again, the individuals must make their own decision. Many times genetic counseling may exacerbate other psychological and social problems within a family and the physician who is giving genetic counseling should be aware of this. If his or her training or skills are not in the area of social and psychological medicine, help should be obtained from other people who have special training, skill, and competence in handling these situations.

MENTAL RETARDATION AND DEAFNESS

"Deafness is one of the treatable causes of mental retardation."* There are two aspects to the problem of hearing loss and mental retardation: the hearing losses which masquerade as mental retardation, and those cases of mental retardation in which a hearing loss exacerbates the retardation.

It is well known that congenitally deaf children will be retarded in their verbal and language ability. Furthermore, if habilitative treatment is not instituted at an early age, the child will appear to be extremely mentally retarded. Many times older children, ages 3 to 10, have been considered to be retarded and/or autistic. These children are sometimes found to have severe to profound hearing losses. A program of habilitation to increase their

*Dr. I. Rapin, personal communication.

hearing ability, either through the use of a hearing aid or an operation, and appropriate educational programs are instituted. After a year or less of such therapy, the child begins to develop his or her intelligence and social potential. The changes in these children are remarkable. These clinical observations strongly suggest that all children considered to be mentally retarded or autistic should have very thorough audiometric examinations. The number of cases of mental retardation and/or autism which are purely secondary to hearing loss are probably few in number, but they are children who can be salvaged.

A much larger problem is the child with mental retardation plus an associated hearing loss. It seems reasonable that a child with mental retardation has diminished ability to overcome a sensory deficit when compared to a normal child. The mentally retarded child, it is hypothesized, has less redundance and diminished plasticity in his cognitive and integrated capacity than a normal child. Thus, a dimunition in sensory input will cause a greater deficit in the mentally retarded child than in the normal child. This appears to be true for hearing and the subsequent development of language and verbal skills.

It has been estimated that from 10% to 25% of all mentally retarded individuals have hearing losses ranging from moderate to profound. Many cases of these hearing losses are correctable, either with a hearing aid or with simple medical and surgical therapy. When these children are identified and treated, there is usually a marked improvement in the child's intelligence; his general ability to understand improves and he can carry out more complex activities. For example, a 9-year-old boy was believed to be severely mentally retarded. He had been in a number of habilitative settings where it was felt he was only possibly trainable. The child was seen by the otolaryngologist because his mother had felt for years that the child had decreased hearing with some fluctuation. Physical examination revealed that the child had a midfacial malformation with a submucosal cleft of the palate. This resulted in a chronic mucoid otitis media and a conductive hearing loss of 40 dB in the speech range. The mucoid otitis was diagnostically confirmed by impedance audiometry and physical examination. Myringotomies were performed and middle ear ventilating tubes were inserted. Postoperatively the child's hearing was normal and he then went back to school. A year later he was classified as educable and has markedly progressed as an educable mentally retarded child. This is a common finding in mentally retarded children with hearing loss. Every child considered mentally retarded should

//Every child considered mentally retarded should have, at the time of diagnosis, a complete hearing evaluation.//

have, at the time of diagnosis, a complete hearing evaluation including impedance audiometry. Later the child should also have yearly audiometric impedance examinations so that moderate hearing losses can be picked up. These hearing losses should be treated so that the child can have maximal hearing to maximize his intellectual potential.

The Deaf and Retarded Child

The problem of the profoundly deaf and mentally retarded child is especially difficult. The first step is to identify those children with severe and profound hearing losses and mental retardation. They will require very special habilitative environments. If they are not identified and treated early, they will never be able to achieve their potential and will live their lives at a lower level of function than that which they are capable of. This is a great detriment to the individual and a waste of society's resources.

METHODS OF EARLY DIAGNOSIS

The most important factor in diagnosing childhood deafness early is the ability to test all infants at risk. A community must have a high-risk registry and a screening program for infants and young children during the first three years of life. The infants and children identified as possibly being high-risk or having a hearing loss are then extensively tested. Determining a hearing loss in an infant, even with the best of present technology, is qualitative. However, habilitative resources—e.g., hearing aids, infant auditory training programs, and teaching sign language—require at this time no more than a qualitative statement as to whether an infant has a moderate, severe, or profound hearing loss. Assessing hearing loss in an infant must be done with a number of different techniques. Different techniques assess the same function, i.e., hearing, but allow for variability in the infant's response and variability in the efficacy of the technique. The three techniques most commonly available and used by our clinics are behavioral audiometry, impedance audiometry with the establishment of the middle ear muscle-reflex threshold, and auditory-evoked potentials.

An infant suspected of having a hearing loss who has failed a hearing screening test should have three behavioral hearing tests. The audiologist must record the number of times the infant does and does not respond to the sound stimulus. After three separate testing sessions, the group taking care of the child will have a much better idea of the child's behavioral ability to react to sound. After the completion of each of the behavioral testing sessions, a complete impedance study is done. This includes measurement of the relative acoustic ohms, the middle ear pressure, a tympanogram, and the threshold of the middle ear muscle reflex at 500, 1000, and 2000 Hz. During the same period when the behavioral and impedance audiometry tests are being done, two separate assessments of auditory-evoked potentials are performed.

After all tests are completed, the information is brought together. A reasonable number of the infants tested will show good inter- and intratest consistency. There are unfortunately a significant number of cases in which the results will vary within and between tests. This is due to both the nature of the tests and to the natural variability of an infant's response to the modalities used. Experience has shown that the test-retest and intratest information is essential for an accurate assessment of the infant's hearing ability.

Special attention should be placed on the information gained from impedance audiometry. Impedance audiometry for one infant was normal except for one day when it showed the infant's test results for a high impedance with a low middle ear pressure and absent middle ear muscle reflex. This information was correlated with the auditory-evoked potential test that was done a few days after the impedance test and showed a hearing loss. Another auditory-evoked response test done two weeks previously may show that hearing loss was present. This inconsistency between the two auditory evoked potential tests can be explained by the presence of otitis media during the second test. This is just one of many ways in which the three tests with routine repeat testing can be used to obtain an accurate assessment of an infant's hearing.

The problem of a progressive hearing loss in an infant or young child is especially important. There have been a number of well documented cases of progressive hearing loss during the first 2 to 3 years of life. The best method of being able to diagnose this type of hearing loss is to pay very careful attention to the parents' history and to realize that the parents are much better observers of their child than the physician is. As the clinician learns to really listen to the parents, he will find that he will occasionally be able to make a diagnosis of early progressive hearing loss in a child. If there is a suspicion of progressive hearing loss, the child should be worked up in the same fashion as the child with congenital hearing loss.

Auditory-evoked response should be used for all individuals in which behavioral hearing testing cannot be adequately performed. Children over 4 years old and most adults will not require auditory-evoked potential testing. It is easier to test these individuals, and they should have a more extensive battery of audiological tests. Again, the principle of test and retest reliability is important. For older children and adults there should be at least two tests of all hearing parameters before a definitive diagnosis is made.

THE PHYSICIAN'S ROLE IN THE TOTAL CARE OF THE DEAF PATIENT

Deafness has been a grossly neglected medical subject for too long. Individuals in various disciplines concerned with deafness—physicians, educators, audiologists, speech therapists, hearing-aid technicians, psychologists, acoustical engineers, linguists—have each seen only a small portion of the total deaf person. This has been to the detriment of deaf people and also to those whose professions deal with the disease of deafness.

An integrated program must be developed for the total management of the deaf individual, especially the deaf

> //A single administrative facility is necessary in which all those activities associated with deafness can be coordinated and related to each individual.//

infant and child. A single administrative facility is necessary in which all those activities associated with the diagnosis, habilitation, treatment and follow-up, and prevention of deafness can be coordinated and related to each individual. It is essential that the various physicians—neurologists, geneticists, pediatricians, otorhinolaryngologists, ophthalmologists—be able to communicate with the educators, audiologists, and others concerned in caring for the deaf individual. The converse is also true. It does little good for the audiologist to note that there is a serous otitis media and have no way to inform the otologist. Even more important are the problems which the educators have with each child. Many times problems in educating will be clarified by an exchange of information among the educator and the audiologist and/or physician. There are physiological constraints upon the educational process that have not been fully explored. It is felt that there are many problems educators find that are not realized by physicians. If these problems can be articulated by the educators, the physician may look for other disease processes or other manifestations of the disease process which would begin to answer the educator's problems.

The ideal arrangement for complete services for the deaf child would be to have the services centered in a medical center. The medical center would have a specialized medical staff to serve the medical problems. Five other important components should also be located and coordinated as part of the administrative group: a hearing diagnostic group, an aural-habilitative group, a preschool auditory treatment group, an acoustical engineering group responsible for hearing aids in addition to the maintenance and development of acoustical instruments, and social workers, psychologists, and psychiatrists. These social and psychiatric services are essential in the management of the patients, especially in today's fragmented and less-than-ideal society.

At the present time in the United States there are still many schools for the deaf in which a large number of deaf children are segregated from the rest of society. Each of these schools should be closely affiliated with a medical center which can supply the resources that the school for the deaf lacks for the total care of the children. The educators and medical personnel should establish a meaningful working arrangement, so that each child may be able to optimize his or her potential.

What is needed today for the care of the deaf child in the United States is coordination of dialogue, dialogue between personnel, and the application of known techniques to provide proper care for the deaf. The care of deaf people has been fragmented not only by each special group which does not communicate with other groups, but also by immature, irrational, and untested educational dogmatism. By this is meant the irrational attachments of oralists to their school and exponents of dactylology (sign language) to their school. It becomes quite evident to the clinician with no special interest in the educational dogmas that the important thing is to teach the child how to communicate. Many of our parents of deaf infants have been advised to teach both sign and oral language. In many instances it has been quite reassuring and gratifying to note an 18-month-old infant interpreting all the words in his or her picture book by sign language. Many times the child has language skills equal to that of a hearing sibling. His language at this time is sign language, but there is no reason why this cannot become more universal as time progresses. The possibility of improving the quality of life for the deaf by the coordination of effort and the eradication of dogma is very real. It should be done!

Part II:
PSYCHOLOGICAL ASPECTS OF DEAFNESS

Untreated deafness alters childhood developmental stages at great cost to a family's emotional health. Dr. Altshuler tells how early treatment can open the way to healthier development.

The Social and Psychological Development of the Deaf Child: Problems and Treatment

KENNETH Z. ALTSHULER

The child who is born deaf is not aware of his handicap. He confronts the tasks of his development with the same unknowing zest as any other infant, lacking only one tool for the job—the not inconsequential one of audition. The tasks to be hurdled do not, at the outset, differ substantially from those for other children, and while deafness alters life's experience, it limits neither intelligence nor the capacities for emotional response and normal growth and maturation. What develops from a child's beginnings depends on a concatenation of factors, some that are inevitable as a consequence of the handicap and some that vary with the child's particular environment.

NORMAL PSYCHOLOGICAL DEVELOPMENT

Descriptions of development vary with the viewer's frame of reference. Physiologically, development rests on a natural maturational timetable—the gradual increase in bulk and musculature and the progressive myelinization of pathways that enable wider central and peripheral nervous system functions to evolve. Socially, development entails the change from an egocentric but helpless animal, ruled by wishes to relieve or satisfy the arousal of appetites and tensions, to a social being who is independent, aware of others and his relationship to them, and able to contain impulses and put off gratifications in a fashion appropriate to what the reality may demand.

What Are the Earliest Signs of Infant Socialization?

We presume (there is no way of being certain) that the infant's psychological state is initially one of undifferentiation. He is at one with the world, unaware of where he ends and the world begins, and his expressions of discomfort magically bring relief. His only tool for adaptation lies in his helplessness and the responses it evokes.

The smiling response appears at about three months. It is a nondiscriminating reaction to objects of a certain size that move toward the infant and stop. Spitz (1959) calls the smiling response one of the organizers of the psyche and considers its appearance a milestone in psychosocial growth. When the child smiles at his mother, he reassures her that he appreciates her caring. The smile evokes further responses from the mother that encourage continued growth.

By seven or eight months another organizer appears: the stranger-anxiety response. The infant now recognizes differences between mother and others. The appearance of this response reflects a step forward in the differentiation between self and others. Up until now, need satisfaction depended on the infant's ability to conjure up the other—the particular devoted and satisfying other—at will, by crying or fussing to express the need. He had no clear sense of object constancy (that objects are permanent and exist when out of the immediate sensory field) nor of the balance of power between him and his mother. From the infant's perspective of primordial omnipotence (or his inability to consider other possibilities), his cry was enough to summon (not request or plead for) the satisfaction required. But appearance of the stranger-anxiety response heralds a shift toward beginning to know that objects have a permanent existence outside his ken, and the infant's disquieting perception of relative size and proportion (Ferenczi, 1950; Spitz, 1959).

During the ensuing period of individuation, about nine to sixteen months, the former total symbiosis with the mother becomes less intense. Because the pre-toddler sees the parent as separate, he begins to use her for "emotional refueling," sliding down her lap, for example, to crawl away, returning to touch her, and then leaving again to re-explore at increasing distances the world around him. The optimal distance between mother and child at this time is one which allows both the refueling and the exploration. Should the mother interrupt or pick up the child out of her need for contact rather than his, she often evokes a good deal of outraged wriggling and screaming (Mahler, 1972).

From this springboard of emotional refueling comes the stage of delegated omnipotence (Ferenczi, 1950). With the gradual realization that he is small and that his wishes alone have no power to control, the child's omnipotence yields—but only slightly. With increased individuation of self acquired through touching home base and then moving away, he now shows an increasing awareness of size relationships with the parent. He begins to delegate the omnipotence he thought was his to his parents, whom he then tries to win or identify with and be like, so that they will serve him well and so that he, by being like them, will regain or retain what power he thinks they have. After the months of active practice in separation, this shift is evidenced by the appearance of active approach and rapprochement behavior (Mahler, 1972). During this period, he wants to know his mother's whereabouts and insists that she share in every new acquisition of skill and experience.

The transition from emotional refueling to delegated omnipotence occurs during the second year. During the next several years, recapturing the delegated omnipotence becomes the entrenched developmental game. It is organized around the child's developing language, biologically programmed to evolve rapidly around the middle of the second year. Language serves not only as the vehicle of self-expression and codification of an increasing number of age-specific interests and observations, but may also be the means, in part, by which the child works through and enforces the long process of separation from his parents. As the child struggles to bend mother to his wishes, she responds to emphasize her separation and to add to his training.

==It is the parents' choice that determines the testing battlefield—the pot, the bed, the dining table, the handling or ordering of objects—and the battle rages or wanes according to the energy of the participants.==

The developmental game waxes: between two and three, the big _me_ appears. Toilet training and socialization attempts evoke negativism, obstinacy, and defiant self-assertion. "Me no do it!" may ring through the household. The child tests and asserts his growing mobility, a considerable aid in materiel and maneuver, and the parents respond. It is the parents' choice that determines the testing battlefield—the pot, the bed, the dining table, the handling or ordering of objects—and the battle rages or wanes according to the energy of the participants.

As the victories are gained and the negativism subsides, around age 4 or 5, imitative identification of the parent of the same sex reaches its height. It brings with it competitive rivalry, wishes for exclusive possession of the parent of the opposite sex, and consequent fears of retaliation, damage and loss—in short, the oedipal complex (Freud, 1910).

Resolution of conflicts during this period, too, depend on the balance of forces and feelings within the family. Introduction to school and broadening of interests outside the immediate family also help the child relinquish such direct competition in favor of finding and building his own life.

Intellectual Development

Intelligence unfolds in a manner parallel to psychosocial development. Before eight to ten months or before object constancy is established, the child has developed such sensorimotor habit patterns as grasping, for example, and has coordinated eye, hand, and mouth movement, the modalities involved in apprehending his experience. He can reproduce these patterns in relation to new and different objects, but there is no means-end behavior: the infant accommodates to new stimulation but does not seek it out. After he establishes object permanence and can form and retain symbols consistently, goal-directed action, active investigation, and trial-and-error behavior begin to appear. At 18 months the child is less bound to his perceptual field; he can manipulate symbols internally and quickly perceives by concrete trial and error that he can use a stick, for example, to retrieve a distant, out-of-reach object (Piaget, 1952; Silverman, 1971).

The ability to combine images into symbols ushers in language and expands intelligence during a child's preconceptual period, 18 months to 4 years. With the aid of mental imagery, the child forms notions about objects he is in contact with, and he attaches these notions to the words he is beginning to use. During this phase he reasons by analogy rather than deduction, and he has little understanding of the immutability of objects, or of time and space. When he views an object from a new perspective, he considers it changed: a ball of clay when flattened, for example, will seem quite different than when round, and a child will apply a different series of analogies to apprehend it than he used before.

From 4 to 7, the child grows in his capacities and becomes more logical and flexible. He can consider multiple relations one at a time, but he cannot generalize them as a whole. Later he can maintain different viewpoints at the same time, and from adolescence on, he becomes capable of using formal reasoning operations to develop hypothetical propositions and the deductive reasoning to support or confute them (Piaget, 1952; Silverman, 1971).

DEAFNESS AND DEVELOPMENT

Environment and Healthy Growth

The physical and emotional climate surrounding a child are the nutritional matrices that permit and support the progressive, parallel growth of social, psychological, physiological, and intellectual functions. Just as an inadequate diet or specific vitamin deficiencies can damage the physiologic substrate and thus alter the timetable of growth, so can the emotional climate retard or enrich the process of psychological maturation. Unduly prolonged or intensive battles with the big <u>me</u> of age 2 or 3 begin to sculpt future character traits of unreasoning rebellion or blind obedience. The absence of a caring relationship, someone to want to please and to be like, can hamper the development of conscience and self-control and yield a personality in which ego is king and impulsive satisfaction of the moment is the guiding rule. The intensity of the child's early fears and rage and the balance of expectations for assuagement or deprivation influence the outcome of the oedipal period. And it is out of all this that the capacity comes for deep and tolerant or brittle and shallow social-sexual relationships.

The bouncing baby is a resilient little creature, built to withstand a variety of hard knocks. And fortunately, the company he enters in usually able to provide an environment that approximates his expectations: parents more or less willing to receive him, who are themselves a combination of assets and limitations; siblings, either curious or hostile; and a physical setting of sufficient food and warmth.

Deafness Alters Developmental Pathways

Deafness is a formidable limitation in a baby's adaptive equipment. Prima facie, deafness must influence the progressive developmental paths outlined above. Precisely how it does is unknown. The exact pathways to mediate its effects, the weight to be assigned to each intermediate avenue, and its absolute, residual influence on a human being are all simply unknown. Whatever the results, they derive from the lack of audition in the child, the effect the handicap has on his family, and the continuous repercussions of these two factors as they may hamper and warp the child's growth.

One aspect of sound is its ability to evoke and convey emotion. The normal child only a few weeks old often quiets down at the comforting sound of his mother's voice. Later, when vacillation between separation and attachment is at its peak, he can evoke reassurance through sound from his unseen mother in a nearby room. Through tone, volume, and other cues, we rely on sound to help define and recognize nuance and affect. We learn that the lack of fit between tone and content may be sarcasm or blunted emotion. We soon learn that the tones in anger or encouragement are different from the tone in tenderness and love. The relation of sound to emotion is clearly an important part of the child's tie with his mother and one omitted in the growth of the deaf child (Altshuler, 1964a; Bowlby, 1958).

Sound is also ubiquitous and omnidirectional. It is the only one of our senses that is not concrete and bound to tangible objects. It conveys innumerable bits of important

and unimportant information. It gives us eyes in back of
our heads, so that without conscious effort or direction we
monitor our surroundings flexibly, discriminating the
meaningful from the trivial, even in our sleep (Altshuler,
1964b). One could write a speculative treatise about how
this aspect of audition influences our development in terms
of providing information, allowing for relaxed awareness,
and determining flexibility in discrimination—of figure from
background particularly—that allows the necessary distance
from raw percepts for the conceptual manipulations and
rearrangements of high-level abstract thought. All these
cognitive attributes afforded by the qualities of sound, the
deaf child does without.

==Without hearing, spontaneous mimicry and spontaneous learning of verbal language are impossible==. As
noted above, language is the vehicle for socialization and
training. It is an important part of the process of
separation-individuation between parent and child and has
traditionally been considered a prerequisite for the
development of object relationships in the human pattern

> //It is questionable whether later efforts
> at replacement of language skills, even
> if successful, can make up for the early
> deficiency in the deaf child.//

(Spitz, 1959). The wisdom of evolution assigned the child's
readiness for developing language to the second year of life,
when he is perched and ready to expand his mobility and
emotional awareness of himself and others; to explore, master,
and order his environment; and to augment rapidly his budding
capacity for logical thought. Time may be crucial for language
emergence. Just as no dose of vitamin D will help an already
rachitic child, so is it questionable whether later efforts at
replacement can fully make up for the early deficiency in the
deaf child.

From the evidence available, it is clear that thinking without verbal language is possible (Furth, 1966; Vernon, 1967). It is also self-evident that the absence of sound does not directly affect the potential for intelligence. Experiments with deaf, language-deprived youngsters show they do not necessarily lag behind the usual timetable of development for certain logical operations (Furth, 1966). To the extent that these operations require the use and manipulation of symbols, the deaf child has the readiness and capacity for language development. Any system of symbols used to order data is a language a deaf child may learn. Ordinary verbal language of whatever nation or time is a well-developed, arbitrary, and conventionally agreed-upon set of symbols. Its usefulness lies in the fact that it is shared among so many and that its structure permits increasing levels of symbolic organization. Thus, verbal language serves as the conventional vehicle for transmitting, ordering, and manipulating information. But it is not the only vehicle possible. And at certain levels of abstraction it, too, becomes too imprecise and must be replaced by another symbolic language—the symbols of physical mathematics, for example.

From the viewpoint of emotional development, a language is necessary for other ends. Its role in communicating emotion has already been discussed. Implicitly, when such communication is interfered with, the bond between parent and child is altered, as are the quality of closeness and the ability to identify feelings clearly. A child's wishes to be like another or to give up something for the love of another are hampered when his perception of that other is ambivalent or fuzzy.

Words or signs also make it possible for a child to substitute smaller units of action for larger ones, as the pointing finger or word for milk replaces the child's gross motor signals of frustration. Used this way, words and signs are a model for the containment of actions. It is probably not accidental that the efflorescence of a child's language is generally concurrent with his parents' efforts to help him attain social control and develop a system of internalized constraints. The hours spent playing with words and building the structure of language themselves may well be structuralizing, the child's way of laying down the model and using it as the means for internalization of the noes and yesses that will develop his self-control and automatize containment of his impulses (Altshuler, 1971).

Effects on Parents and Family

Deafness is generally an invisible handicap for the first few months of life. Infant babbling is normal and the smiling response appears on schedule. Somewhere in the second half of the first year, parents begin to be concerned; the babbling falls off, the child is somehow "not right," not responsive in some expected way. One quarter of the time or more, the first doctor consulted denies the possibility of deafness and finds nothing wrong (Schlesinger, 1969).

When the diagnosis is made and finally confirmed, the parents are already anxious and uncertain. Confirmation only makes them feel worse. The physician, misled by his wish to help, often ignorant of what the handicap entails, and uncomfortable in the face of his own uncertainty, may offer reassurance that it is more wishful than accurate: "Hearing aids do wonders" or "He'll be the same as you and I." Frequently, he does not resolve the question of etiology, leaving open the question of whose fault it is.

Parental reaction to the confirmed diagnosis is inevitably depression. Nothing quite matches the creative scope of giving new life, and creation of a child is imbued with all the unresolved fantasies and wishes of one's own early development. To the mother, pregnancy is quite often a fulfillment, a restoration wished for as disproof of any previous deficiencies—hence her inordinate concern that everything be all right. For the father, creation of new life is also an extension of self and a demonstration of primeval potency. The presence of a defect in their baby is a blow to the parents, and they react to deafness in proportion to the intensity of their aspirations (Lax, 1972).

> //Depression is inevitable, and parents react to it with wishes of denial—magical hopes of cure, magical expectations of hearing aids, magical wishes with regard to speech training.//

Depression is inevitable, and parents react to it with wishes of denial—magical hopes of cure, magical expectations of hearing aids, magical wishes with regard to speech training. They filter and refract through their hopes for normalcy all advice received. They may bend out of all proportion the frequent injunction to encourage speech by avoidance of gestures, thus becoming wooden indians, mobile only at the lips, yet attempting to express warmth to their child; or they become pretzel-like, uncomfortable contortionists as they strive to be natural with their mouths down at the eye level of a two-foot infant!

But wishful denial cannot work, and the deafness does not go away. Its presence is an unavoidable reminder of possible personal failure and disappointed aspirations. The parental dilemma is how to love a child who represents such a reminder. The handicap evokes anger because it is an unsolvable problem. The anger threatens to spill over to the child, in turn eliciting and enhancing guilt about responsibility for the handicap. Parents express this melange of feelings as confused, ambivalent behavior toward their child. The parent hopes the child will be no different from others, follows overscrupulously each directive that promises aid, resents the need to do so and the reminder of difference that such efforts pose, becomes oversolicitous to cover and make up for the resentment, and becomes confused in the face of his own feelings and the uncertainty of how to relate to a child different from the norm--all without knowing just what the difference really means for the future.

It is unfortunate that parents must go through this confusion at a time when the child's own battle between separation-individuation is also at its peak. To force the eye contact necessary for communication, parents will often grab the child's face, interfering with his efforts at independent activity. The space or optimal distance between parent and child is thus narrowed, while the language and sound which would provide reassurance and the optimal distance are missing between the two. The results may border on the bizarre as the child's anxiety and the mother's overconcern heighten the coercive need for attachment between the two. Often there are prolonged temper tantrums on both sides as both react to social requirements without the expressive vehicle of language. Power struggles with the big me often intensify, and more often than not, it is the parents who capitulate, allowing the child to become neglected or a tyrant, confused in awareness of self and others, misunderstanding and misunderstood.

In sum, the child's lack of audition frequently yields a limited ability to communicate and apprehend that emotionality which is integral to a child's bond with his mother and a mode for the expression and development of love, closeness, and individuation. A late and limited development of language attenuates a deaf child's chances to form those aspects of abstraction involving symbolic recall, recognition of similarities, and deduction of consequences. On the parental side, there is depression, resentment, guilt, and ambivalence. And each intrudes and impinges upon the line and quality of the child's timetable for growth (Altshuler, 1968; Bruner, 1961; Levine, 1960; Shirley, 1933).

Entering the World Outside

The deaf child enters the world outside his family somewhere between ages 3 and 6, depending on the availability of special preschool facilities nearby or the need to wait for kindergarten at a school for deaf children. ==Once in school, the language lag dominates his education.== It demands untold hours of general teaching and speech training to get a basic curriculum across to the child. The results cannot be considered optimal, for the average youngster leaves his special school at age 18 with about a fourth-to-fifth-grade proficiency in reading and mathematics. ==Only about one-quarter of deaf students develop speech usable for easy social intercourse with others in the world.==

Moreover, because it takes so much time and effort to spoon-feed basic information, a deaf child may come to expect that everything must be done for him; such a dependent attitude stultifies more free-wheeling, creative, and independent thought. In this connection, it has been observed that deaf youngsters of 13 and 14 continue longer than their hearing counterparts to blame others for their misdeeds and to lack the camaraderie and mutual interest typical of hearing adolescents (Sarlin and Altshuler, 1968). Learning by rote, they often also lack, even at older ages, a depth of awareness for the reasons and their interplay that underly roles in dating and family behavior, aspirations for further education, or rules of job responsibility. That these attitudes can be modified has been shown in experiments where groups of deaf youngsters were stimulated to be more mutually aware and give closer scrutiny to the feelings of and for each other, from which develop a later sense of interpersonal and community responsibility (Rainer and Altshuler, 1970).

Families, too, continue to have a difficult time. Imagine the mixture of feelings evoked for child and parent when the deaf child at animated dinner conversations must limit his participation to some variation of "Please pass the potatoes." Or again, imagine the logistic difficulties in planning such a simple family event as going to the movies with a deaf youngster whose lack of comprehension may mean boredom and disturbing activity. Experience indicates also that families go through a recrudescence of their earlier depression during the child's adolescence. At this point, the deaf child can no longer depend on his physical ability at games to maintain his social position; his hearing peers spurt ahead in social development, and he is excluded. This relative lagging behind makes untenable his family's remaining efforts to deny or minimize the difference (Rainer and Altshuler, 1970).

PSYCHIATRIC PROBLEMS OF THE DEAF CHILD

Incidence and Causes

In view of the above, it seems nothing short of miraculous that the majority of deaf children turn out to be normal neurotics like the rest of us. Clinical studies of adult psychiatric patients indicate that the major forms of psychotic illness are no more frequent for the deaf person than for the hearing person (Altshuler, 1968, 1971, Altshuler and Sarlin, 1962; Grinker et al, 1971; Rainer et al, 1969). Mental illness in deaf patients shows only modifications of presentation and form, and problems of impulse control appear to be more common. Unfortunately, there is no psychiatric hospital in the country geared to study the special problems of deaf, disturbed children. As a consequence, comparable reports on prevalence and types of illness, let alone their prognoses, do not exist, and we have to rely on the impressions of clinical experience.

Additional Handicaps

We have traced the developmental path of the normal child with early total deafness. For the sake of discussion, we have assumed that deafness was the sole handicap. Genetic causes underlie early total deafness in roughly half the persons affected; an additional 10 to 15 percent are deaf from pre- or perinatal influences, and the remainder from later, exogenous causes (Rainer et al, 1969). Other handicaps, from mild to severe, may appear when maternal rubella, meningitis or encephalitis is in the patient's history. In such cases developmental problems are compounded. Resultant difficulties complicate observed behavior and pose obstacles for diagnosis and treatment in the first two categories of illness to be discussed.

The group of childhood psychoses, comprising infantile autism and childhood schizophrenia, are rare. The clinical picture shows grossly abberant development, poor attention span, excessive clinging or twirling, and lack of social relatedness. The consensus is that these disturbances come from a variety of causes, ranging from gross organic damage, which may spare potential for intelligence while striking hard at the ability to coordinate and integrate perception of self and outside, through barely perceptible organic residuals, to illness attributable to severely disturbed patterns of mothering. Most of these disturbances are well established before age five. The rarer case develops from latency to preadolescence and may resemble the more classical schizophrenia, in which one can mark the turning point from normal development to withdrawal or uncontrolled behavior, and a demonstrable thought disorder is present.

It is important to differentiate the weight of any organic contribution in all cases, to avoid imposing an additional burden of guilt on already buffeted parents. Accurate diagnosis generally entails comprehensive physical, neurological, and psychiatric evaluation. What to do after establishing a diagnosis is generally a difficult question. Treatment is always a problem, for there is no facility especially prepared to receive these children, and only a few psychiatrists have shown a particular interest in them. Often, if behavior is not too disruptive, the best course is to retain the child in a school for deaf children, with supervision by the school's mental health team and consultation with an outside psychiatrist. If his behavior becomes too disruptive, however, the child finds his way to the childrens' unit in a mental hospital or a school for the retarded. While no statistics are available, it is clear that the prognosis is poor.

A second related but more common group of problems may be designated as expressions of motivation versus capacity. The symptoms may be indistinguishable from those of the behavioral disorders (discussed below), but arise in the child with a mild, often masked, multiple handicap, such as minimal brain dysfunction or below-normal intelligence. To guide him to the underlying extra handicap, the examiner records a careful history showing when the child began lagging behind in normal development—eg, sitting up, walking, or grasping. Then the child undergoes psychological testing for hand-eye coordination and motor function, as well as for intellectual ability.

With minimal brain dysfunction or mild intellectual impairment, the child may not be able to meet normal educational and social demands; he reacts with a host of behavioral symptoms. The slow child improves when others reduce their expectations of what he must do. Remedial training helps the child with perceptual motor problems. In cases of hyperactivity secondary to minimal brain disorder, the use of amphetamines or the phenothiazines may quiet the child sufficiently so that he can maintain school progress and minimize his secondary emotional difficulties until he has matured to sustaining better control. Of course the family must take part in the proceedings from the beginning. They need counseling at each stage to understand causes, reasons, the role of their own expectations, and the ultimate prognosis. Parents also require supportive psychotherapy and guidance for a time by one knowledgeable in child development.

By far, the most common and widespread type of disturbance is the childhood behavior disorder, which, more often than not, turns out to be a problem of family as well. In attempting to understand these problems, we should remind ourselves that the young child is, after all, an immature organism. He reacts to stress through only a limited number of outlets. Thus, such symptoms as hyperactivity, irritability, withdrawal, aggression, sleeping disturbances, and eating problems may be the result of a variety of different causes. The symptoms are common outlets the child uses to relieve tension built up by unresolved conflicts. Rarely are symptoms specific for a particular underlying cause; the entire repertoire may result from any of a wide gamut of tension-evoking circumstances.

Indeed, it is the rare child who never displays any of these symptoms sometime during his growth. If his nightmares, tantrums, or fears of the dark, for example, are transient or circumscribed and do not affect his social or other areas of development, they should probably be considered normal concomitants of growth, temporary outlets for overload of one kind or another. If they persist or interfere with social and educational aspects of the child's life, parents must take them more seriously, as a call for understanding and treatment.

The Deaf Child's Role in Family Conflicts

It is hardly surprising that such difficulties seem to be quite common among deaf children. In addition to other problems

> //The child's silence makes him a likely screen on which the core of a family neurosis may be projected or played out. He may thus become the center of a power struggle.//

confronting parents and child, the simple fact of the child's silence makes him a likely screen on which the core of a family neurosis may be projected or played out. He may thus become the center of a power struggle between parents, or be viewed as the cause of their own internecine difficulties. For an otherwise undirected, empty parent, his needs may become the reason for being—a heavy responsibility for a small child. He can be assigned the central role in a parent's demonstration of ambitions to rescue and provide, or he can serve as a focus of hidden bias.

==Behavior disorders ignored in early years can evolve into adult neuroses or warped character structures.== Not uncommonly, parents hold unwarranted convictions of a child's stupidity or ineptitude, or attempt frenetic efforts to deny his normal limitation (Rainer, 1966).

DENIAL AT WORK

One 17-year-old, seen for depression and tantrums, was caught in a conflict over choosing to go to college or a trade school. Because of their own high intellectual and status aspirations, his parents had largely overestimated the boy's communication skills and intelligence, neither of which was adequate for college work. Their persistent denial that his deafness was a factor to be considered finally led the boy to become utterly convinced that deaf people were inferior. Because he shared his parents' aspirations, he could neither mingle with other deaf youngsters as an equal nor accept himself with any genuine appreciation of what his real assets were.

Some of these family attitudes came to light only when the parents were pressed about why they had consistently forbidden the boy to learn manual language. Finally, their feelings came out: they were afraid that their son's communicating manually would put him in bad company—other deaf people. They also thought that the manual language itself was dirty and disgusting. While it was possible to help in this particular situation, cases tackled so late can sometimes end in failure.

A family's investment in long-held attitudes can lead them to abort any treatment effort and to rationalize their refusal to continue by citing a therapist's lack of understanding and the "uncooperativeness" of the agency.

Earlier efforts generally bear better fruit, and problems in the nascent state often are solvable. One young mother, talking in a group setting, told how she daily dressed her deaf son, aged 4, while her hearing daughter, aged 2-1/2, dressed herself. When members of the group and the leader raised some questions, she saw that she had exaggerated the hearing handicap to one of almost total helplessness.

==If parents cannot prevent behavioral difficulties or if they do not subside in a reasonable time, psychiatric help should be sought.== And it should be clear from the above that such help must always involve the other important family members. Behavior disorders in children are eminently treatable; when undue pressures are relieved, the child's natural resiliency and ability to grow generally drift back again towards the straight developmental line.

A DOSE OF REALITY

A young mother came to a supervised group session. She was full of guilt and self-loathing for having an imperfect child. When other young mothers in her neighborhood asked questions about when her child sat, stood, or how many teeth it had, she misinterpreted the questions as vicious and meddlesome probing, designed "to put me down." She could not consider another possibility: that the mothers asked such questions only to reassure themselves of their own child's developmental timetable. Instead, she felt each question was pointed toward telling her she had a freak instead of a child. Indeed, they did, for this was her own conviction. She began to isolate herself in indignation from all her neighbors, a reaction clearly fraught with danger for herself and for her child's development. When the group leader and several of the other mothers present emphasized the reality, she gradually began to see some of her own feelings and their consequences. She finally reacted with an enlightened horror at herself and, as the basically good lady she was, began to reopen her lines of friendship with other mothers and to reevaluate her feelings toward the child.

Deaf Children of Deaf Parents

Problems of deafness were discussed earlier as if deaf people were a homogeneous group. Of course, this is not true. In addition to the number of deaf children with additional handicaps, there is further heterogeneity if the deaf children are considered from the standpoints of age of onset of deafness, socioeconomic background of their families, and the like. Aside from the obvious advantages in language development that accrue when deafness comes on at a later age, such subclassifications have little bearing on psychological factors. But while the vast majority of deaf youngsters are born to hearing parents, about 10 percent have two deaf parents. This particular group warrants special mention because of a number of findings.

Deaf children of deaf parents are frequently described as better adjusted (Brill, 1960; Rainer et al, 1969). Some studies comparing them with deaf children of hearing parents show that they have a higher educational level, better command of language, and higher reading scores in finger-spelling and vocabulary (Stevenson, 1964; Stuckless and Birch, 1966). Other investigations show that they score higher on achievement tests and on teacher ratings for characteristics of maturity, responsibility, independence, sociability, and appropriate sex-role behavior. Reports also rate them higher for facility in written language, receptive and expressive finger-spelling, absence of communicative frustration, and willingness to communicate with strangers; all of this with no difference from other deaf children in speech- and lip-reading ability (Meadow, 1967, 1969; Quigley, 1966).

Schlesinger (1969) aptly summarizes these findings:

> Clinical studies, experimental evidence, and anecdotal material indicate that the interaction of deaf parents and their deaf children may be

markedly different from that of hearing parents and their deaf children. These differences in interaction may be traced to influences of reaction to diagnosis, with subsequent coping mechanisms affecting patterns of child rearing and early parent-child communication.

Deaf parents of deaf children appear to expect the diagnosis and to accept it at a much earlier age. (They) cope with the crisis of diagnosis more easily and quickly, while their hearing counterparts prolong and intensify it. Even following the diagnosis, deaf parents appear to be more comfortable with their deaf children, admit to fewer eating and toilet training problems, and permit earlier independence and autonomy. Once the initial diagnosis is made, deaf parents are less likely to seek confirmatory diagnosis or a miraculous cure.

Early parent-child communication is a traumatic issue between hearing parents and their deaf children. Although the hearing parents talk to and in front of the child, they can only guess at his level of understanding. Although the child may watch carefully and understand the nonverbal messages, he does not know the symbols, the words his parents use until much later, and he cannot reproduce them.

Most deaf parents, however, use sign language with their deaf and hearing children. Deaf parents, as they communicate to and in front of the child, can test the child's understanding more easily. The child, watching carefully, can learn the symbols, the signs the parents use, and learn to understand and reproduce them more easily. These deaf children may be the only ones who learn a language naturally, playfully, as a "mother tongue". They may also be the only deaf children who learn language at a very early age which may indeed be the critical age (my italics).

We have laid the special difficulties of the deaf child to these facts: he does not hear the cues for emotion transmitted by sound; he does not learn verbal language at the optimal time; and his handicap is the starting point for a vicious circle of maladaptive influences, as parental reaction influences him, and his responses in behavior evoke further maladaption.

The deaf children of deaf parents are not paragons of mental health, and deafness remains a handicap which alters and influences their life experience (Blackmore, 1971). Nonetheless, the evidence suggests that they do fare better in a number of ways. Clearly, the reasons must be the relative lack of parental discomfort in the presence of deafness and the greater freedom and earlier development of communication between parent and child.

Healthier Development

The fact that audition is unavailable as an agent evocateur for cues to evoke emotional expression cannot be made up for in the deaf child. Nor can audition's role as transmitter of distant information from all directions at once be replaced. What can be minimized are the effects of the relative absence of language, and the effects of parental response to the presence of a handicap.

Communication Without Language

Unfortunately, these two effects are not often clearly separable, partly because parents and professionals, as well, tend to confuse language and communication with words and oral speech. The average hearing child learns language spontaneously and seems to generate for himself the rules of syntax and grammar. By age 5 he has linguistic competence and his vocabulary ranges from 5,000 to 26,000 words (Lenneberg, 1967). Comparable data are not available for the deaf child, but he is generally woefully behind. Recent

> //The deaf child of deaf parents develops vocabulary and communication skills in signs that are equal to the competence of his hearing peers.//

investigations of the first year or two of life indicate that the deaf child of deaf parents develops vocabulary and communication skill in signs that equals the competence of his hearing peers (Schlesinger and Meadow, 1971).

From the psychological and developmental view, it is the communication and understanding that is important rather than and not its form (Rainer, 1966; Rainer et al, 1969). Signs, writing, gestures, speech—everything that enhances clarity and communicative comprehension—should be invoked if genuine two-way understanding is to come about. As part of this understanding, parents must recognize and accept how their child may be different from them and utilize what is most natural for him. The language of signs has an advantage in that it has a structure that can be learned easily at a mother's knee, where she can introduce comparable rules of syntax and grammar in a natural, age-specific fashion, thereby providing and expanding the base of language at the appropriate time. A child knowledgeable in signs probably has the framework already present to be able to learn verbal English, written if not spoken, with the same transfer of knowledge that a hearing child makes use of when he learns a second verbal language.

==Training in sign language is not meant to be an alternative to oral training, but an adjunct and supplement.== Parents should be informed that they must use every method of communication early and consistently. They should speak to their deaf child and encourage the use of voice and words; but they should also learn fingerspelling and manual language, and employ both voice and hands from the beginning. It is over this point that one usually encounters the psychological problems of parents, especially their wishes to deny the handicap. As in most spurious arguments, too crusading an espousal of either the manual or oral cause usually rests on layers of anxiety and negation.

Tapping the Resources

How is one to overcome these problems and where should the responsibility lie? Obviously, the physician who makes the diagnosis is the first way station. General practitioners, otolaryngologists, and audiologists should go beyond diagnosis alone to find out about deafness and its consequences and about the difficulties parents have in dealing with the handicap. They must counsel parents about the facts; disabuse them gently and over time about any notions for absolute normality; point out that only a few deaf children develop excellent speech; and that there is no way of predicting which child will succeed. They must emphasize the need for language and open communication by whatever avenue and tell them what they can learn from the studies of children of deaf parentage. Parents must be helped in recovering from their depressions and assisted in overcoming their ambivalence; they must be made to see that the effects of the handicap to their child can be minimized only by a realistic appraisal of him, by their dealing with him as he is, not as they wish him to be. They must understand the limitations as well as the value of hearing aids.

Psychiatric referrals must be made freely, for it is part of the psychiatrist's function to give the time in listening and lending aid that the general practitioner has only in short supply. Psychiatric work with parents helps them to recognize their own feelings and how the reflection of these feelings in behavior may be more damaging than helpful. Such awareness can help them avoid painful situations such as those just mentioned. As knowledge is the master of superstition, families should be encouraged to meet with other parents of deaf children of all ages to see firsthand what variety life can give. They should be advised to read this book and such other works as They Grow in Silence, by Mindel and Vernon; Our Deaf Children, by Freddy Bloom, and In This Sign, by Joanne Greenberg, all of which will deepen their understanding of deafness and help replace exaggerated fears with realistic appraisal. The Deafness Annual, published by the Professional Rehabilitation Workers with the Adult Deaf, Washington, DC, is a useful source of programs available to deaf people and a guide to where parents can obtain sign-language training.

None of these measures will remove the handicap. The deaf child is deaf and will always be so. By opening communication and enhancing the development of language on its age-specific schedule, and by coming to accept only realistic limitations, not the excessive ones that personal fantasies may have engendered, parents can enable the deaf child to grow to maturity and intelligence as a productive, responsible and reasonably well-adjusted adult.

REFERENCES

Altshuler KZ: Personality traits and depressive symptoms in the deaf, in Wortis J (ed.): Recent Advances in Biological Psychiatry. New York, Plenum Publishing Corporation, 1964a

Altshuler KZ: Snoring: Unavoidable nuisance or psychological symptoms. Psychoanal Q, 33: 552, 1964b

Altshuler KZ: Reaction to and management of sensory loss: Blindness and deafness, in Schoenberg B, et al (eds.): Loss and Grief. New York, Columbia University Press, 1968

Altshuler KZ: Studies of the deaf: Relevance to psychiatric theory. Am J Psychiatry, 127: 11, 1971

Altshuler KZ, Sarlin MB: Deafness and schizophrenia: Interrelation of communication stress, maturation lag and schizophrenic risk, in Kallmann FJ (ed.): Expanding Goals in Genetics in Psychiatry. New York, Grune & Stratton, Inc, 1962

Blackmore HJ: The deaf child can never be normal, in Occasional Papers. East Melbourne, Australian Association of Welfare Officers to the Deaf, 1971, no 2

Bloom F: Our Deaf Children, Heinemann Ltd, London; Milbourne, Toronto, 1963

Bowlby J: The nature of the child's tie to his mother. Int J Psychoanal, 39: 350, 1958

Brill RG: A study in the adjustment of three groups of deaf children. Except Child, 26: 464, 1960

Bruner JS: Cognitive consequences of early sensory deprivation, in Solomon P, et at (eds.): Sensory Deprivation. Cambridge, Mass, Harvard University Press, 1961

Ferenczi S: Stages in the development in the sense of reality, in Selected Papers of Sandor Ferenczi. New York, Basic Books, Inc, Publishers, 1950, vol 1

Freud S: Introductory lectures on psychoanalysis, in Standard Edition of the Complete Psychological Works of Sigmund Freud. London, The Hogarth Press Ltd, 1910, vol 11

Furth HG: Thinking Without Language. New York, The Free Press of Glen Cove, Inc, 1966

Greenberg J: In This Sign. New York, Holt, Rinehart, and Winston, Inc, 1970

Grinker RR Sr, et al: Psychiatric Diagnosis, Therapy, and Research on the Psychotic Deaf. Washington, DC, US Department of Health, Education and Welfare, Social and Rehabilitation Service, 1971

Lax RF: Some aspects of the interaction between mother and impaired child. Mother's narcissistic trauma. Int J Psychoanal, 53: 339, 1972

Lenneberg EH: The Biological Foundations of Language. New York, John Wiley & Sons, Inc, 1967

Levine ES: The Psychology of Deafness. New York, Columbia University Press, 1960

Mahler MS: On the first three subphases of the separation-individuation process. Int J Psychoanal, 53: 833, 1972

Meadow KP: The Effects of Early Manual Communication and Family Climate on the Deaf Child's Development, unpublished PhD dissertation. University of California, 1967

Meadow KP: Self image family climate and deafness. Social Forces, 47: 428, 1969

Mindel E, Vernon, M: They Grown in Silence. The Deaf Child and His Family. Silver Spring, Md, National Association of the Deaf, 1971

Norris AG, Lloyd GT (ed): Deafness Annual, 11: Washington, DC, Professional Rehabilitation Workers With the Adult Deaf, 1972

Piaget J: The Origins of Intelligence in Children. New York, International Universities Press, 1952

Quigley S: The problems of communication of deaf children, in What is Special Education? Proceedings International Conference. Middlesex, England, Association for Special Education, 1966

Rainer JD: Interpretation, communication, and understanding. The Deaf American, 19: 43, 1966

Rainer JD, Altshuler KZ, Kallmann FJ: Family and Mental Health Problems in a Deaf Population, ed 2, Springfield, Ill, Charles C Thomas, Publisher, 1969

Rainer JD, Altshuler KZ: Expanded Mental Health Care for the Deaf: Rehabilitation and Prevention. New York, New York State Psychiatric Institute, 1970

Sarlin MB, Altshuler KZ: Group psychotherapy with deaf adolescents in a school setting. Int J Group Psychother, 18: 337, 1968

Schlesinger HS: The deaf pre-schooler and his many faces, in Lloyd G (ed.): International Seminar of the Vocational Rehabilitation of Deaf Persons. Washington, DC, US Department of Health, Education, and Welfare, 1969

Schlesinger HS, Meadow KP: Deafness and Mental Health: A Developmental Approach. Langley Porter Neuropsychiatric Institute, San Francisco. Social and Rehabilitation Service, Washington, DC, 1971

Shirley MM: The First Two Years. Minn, University of Minnesota Press, 1933

Silverman MA: The growth of logical thinking: Piaget's contribution to ego psychology. Psychoanal Q, 15: 317, 1971

Spitz RA: A Genetic Field Theory of Ego Formation. New York, International Universities Press, 1959

Stevenson EA: A study of the educational achievements of deaf parents. Calif, The California News, 80: 143, 1964

Stuckless ER, Birch JW: The influence of early manual communication on linguistic development of deaf children. Am An Deaf, 3: 452, 1966

Vernon M: Relationship of language to the thinking process. Arch Gen Psychiatry, 16: 325, 1967

When the outcome of pregnancy disappoints parents, how do they react? Dr. Vernon suggests ways for physicians to cope constructively with parents' feelings.

Psychological Aspects in Diagnosing Deafness in a Child*

McCAY VERNON

Parents of deaf children tend to have hostile feelings toward physicians and other professionals who diagnose their child's deafness (Hefferman, 1955; Mindel and Vernon, 1972). Obviously, part of the hostility grows out of the disappointment and frustration these parents feel over their child's handicap. The remainder stems from the tendency of parents to endow the physician with a power to heal greater than medical science and then to blame him when a miracle cure is not forthcoming.

Fortunately, research on the psychodynamics of parents at the time they discover their child's deafness yields data of great value to the physician who must make such a diagnosis and communicate it to the family. The psychodynamics are of vital, often permanent, consequence

*This article originally appeared in Eye, Ear, Nose and Throat Monthly, Volume 52, February, 1973. Reproduced by permission.

to the family and the child. The physician's constructive counsel at this time of trauma can avoid irreversible psychological damage and inappropriate family reactions, which can be more devastating to the child than deafness itself.

What follows is a description of the basic family psychodynamics which surround the diagnosis of deafness along with suggestions for the physician on how to cope with these feelings in a constructive manner for all concerned. This discussion traces the etiology and development of parental dynamics, starting with pregnancy.

PREGNANCY: A TIME OF AMBIVALENCE

Pregnancy often occurs at a time when parents are not ready or do not want it. Even couples who desire and plan for a pregnancy have ambivalent feelings about it. On the one hand, they have high expectations and hopes; they may develop feelings of fulfillment and family closeness. On the other hand, they also may resent the added responsibility, the disfigurement, and the demands. Sometimes one spouse blames the other for the carelessness that led to conception.

> //Ambivalent feelings and fantasies are widespread in even normal parents and have tremendous implications for the feelings of guilt and denial which occur later if the child is diagnosed as deaf.//

These mixed feelings inevitably result in some wishful fantasies that the pregnancy may end prematurely. The pregnant woman may deliberately violate clearly understood rules of prenatal care, such as carrying heavy loads of laundry, riding horseback, taking very hot baths, or engaging in other inappropriate physical activity. She may make more direct attempts to abort, involving quinine, probing of the uterus, or drinking turpentine. While rarely mentioned in professional literature, such cases are well known by obstetricians and psychotherapists who work with young parents. Thus, ambivalent feelings and fantasies are widespread even in "normal" parents. These feelings and fantasies have tremendous implications for the feelings of guilt and denial which occur later if their child is diagnosed as deaf.

THE EARLY YEARS: DELAY COMPOUNDS CONFUSION

Generally, one to three years go by before deafness is discovered. Part of the reason for this delay is that few infants have total hearing losses. Most respond to the gross sounds of airplanes roaring overhead, motors backfiring, and pots and pans banging. This masks their inability to understand speech sounds. The inability to hear speech well enough to understand it is what deafness is.

Even though parents delay the actual discovery of deafness, they generally sense something wrong before they receive the diagnosis. For example, they miss the infant's subtle responses and reactions to sound that are basic to the mothering process. Parental expectations are often unfulfilled because the baby shows little responsiveness or is so slow in some areas of development, such as language and speech.

Gradually, anxiety increases. The mother may wonder if the child is retarded. Questions start to arise, such as, "Why doesn't my child talk?" or "Is something wrong? Our baby does not talk." Because these kinds of expressions of anxiety are rather common among mothers of normal children, physicians and others may understandably pass them off with comments such as, "He'll grow out of it," "Everything is fine; now just don't worry," or "Just give him time."

While these comments may temporarily, albeit falsely,

allay concern, before long they arouse increasing frustration, confusion, and anxiety in the family. The parents realize something is drastically wrong, yet their questions are essentially ignored, and they often are given contrary-to-fact information.

Failure to confirm the diagnosis of deafness has two serious impacts. First, it delays habilitation past a period some believe is crucial in the psychological and educational development of the child; second, it arouses confusion, anxiety, fear, anger, and guilt feelings in the parents. Such feelings cannot be constructively channeled toward the resolution of the child's disturbance until the family finds out what the problem is.

The Danger of Misdiagnosis

While failure to detect deafness is bad enough, far worse is misdiagnosis, which occurs to at least one third of parents with deaf children (Mindel and Vernon, 1971). Misdiagnosis may be the outcome of a complex problem of differential diagnosis between brain damage, aphasia, delayed speech, autism, childhood schizophrenia, mental retardation, and deafness.

Instances of misdiagnosis are documented. One psychologist reports that in his own private practice, he found 15 deaf persons who were not retarded in institutions for the mentally retarded. One was the daughter of an ophthalmologist, who was sent to a hospital for the retarded when she was 2 and spent five years there. Another boy, now in college, spent three years in the same hospital. A recent deaf graduate student at Western Maryland College once spent two years in a facility for the retarded.

The most serious misdiagnoses usually are made in cases of multiply handicapped deaf children, those who have profound hearing losses and cerebral palsy, vestibular pathology, or some other additional disability.

While diagnostic difficulties may make the error of misdiagnosis more understandable, the results are more destructive because they compound the difficulties of a child already doubly handicapped. However, certainly not all misdiagnosed or undiagnosed deaf children are multiply handicapped. While physicians most often misdiagnose deafness, some of the greatest errors are made by psychologists who give verbal tests to nonverbal deaf children, an unpardonable mistake.

Taking Action on Early Warning Signals

The major point is that a child's delayed speech or apparent failure to respond to sound should never be ignored, nor should a diagnosis be attempted until his hearing has been thoroughly tested audiologically.

Usually either parents or the doctor discover deafness, but sometimes outsiders are the first to notice; even then, parents—especially the more accepting ones—may be a long time in taking the possibility seriously.

This delayed awareness can be the first manifestation of the parents unconscious denial of deafness. Often in interviews, parents can recall observing the symptoms of deafness in their child but claim never to have associated these with hearing loss. For example, the mother may say, "Mary did not respond to my voice," "Ann was disobedient," "Frank slept with the vacuum cleaner on," or "He slept through the fireworks on the Fourth of July."

THE DIAGNOSIS OF DEAFNESS: ITS IMPACT ON PARENTS

By the time deafness is finally diagnosed, the child is usually in his second or third year. For some parents, confirmation brings initial feelings of relief, especially if they have previously been told their child was retarded, autistic, or had some other problem they thought worse than deafness. However, to most families, the discovery of deafness is a traumatic blow, the full depth of which the bearer of the news rarely senses. It is common for parents to say, "I do not remember a thing the doctor said after I was told my child was deaf."

Coping With Irreversibility: Acceptance or Denial

There has been excellent medical research on how families cope with the discovery that they have a child with a serious, irreversible disability. Hamburg (1953), Cholden (1958), and others (Grinker, 1969; Siller, 1969) establish several general principles crucial in making the diagnosis of deafness and communicating it to the family.

One principle is that constructive and effective coping with a permanent disability begins only after the patient and family are fully aware of its irreversibility and its total implications. As long as hope is extended for a possible cure or some indication given that the ramifications of the disability can be overcome, patients and their families do not adjust to the reality of deafness and the resulting new life circumstances.

> //Only when and if a person realizes exactly what changes he will have to make in his life can the kinds of adaptations that are effective become possible.//

Only when and if a person realizes exactly what changes he will have to make in his life can the kinds of adaptations that are effective become possible. This generalization holds true for all disabled individuals and is a fundamental premise upon which all rehabilitation begins. It places tremendous responsibility upon the professional who informs parents that their child is deaf—a responsibility for which most are unprepared.

Another principle derived from research on reaction to disability is that certain defenses or coping procedures are almost universal. The most important defense is initial denial of the defect or denial of its implications.

Denial and Deafness: Who Denies It and Why

Studies of parents of leukemic children and of blind persons (Hamburg, 1953; Cholden, 1958) show that denial is a normal coping mechanism through which human beings initially protect themselves at a time of trauma. It is when denial becomes chronic that it is pathological and prevents constructive adjustment to disability.

At the time a child is discovered to be deaf, parents typically deny it. For example, parents with pre-school children usually sense something different in their deaf child within his first year, but they rarely deal with this awareness directly. Sometimes grandparents, relatives, or neighbors finally force the parents to face the fact that their child is deaf. Even after parents identify, acknowledge, and want to do something about deafness, the physician often tells them that the child will grow out of it or that everything is going to be all right (Mindel and Vernon, 1971). Thus there seems to be almost a conspiracy of denial on the part of parents and the professional community (Mindel and Vernon, 1971).

When the diagnosis is confirmed, the power of denial becomes more vivid; no longer is it the blatant rejection of deafness per se, but the more subtle and destructive denial of the implications of profound hearing loss.

Generally, parents do not receive an explanation about the full implications of deafness (Grinker, 1969; Mindel and Vernon, 1971). In some cases they learn almost nothing about what deafness will mean in the life of their child and the family. Parents may be told only that their child is deaf and that they should go home and wait until he is old enough to attend school.

On occasion, the audiologist or physician who diagnoses the deafness also informs the parents, but tells them that a hearing aid, speech lessons, and lipreading instruction will be provided. This can be helpful. The danger is that parents are often led to believe that prostheses and training are going to enable the child to function as though he were not deaf. When parents are informed of deafness, rarely are they given time to really sit down and talk about it or to work through the very intense feelings that arise on this occasion and which will persist over the weeks and months ahead.

How Professionals Deny Deafness

Thus, there are several crucially important occurrences that take place at the time of diagnosis and in the period that follows. First, the professional with whom the parents are in contact frequently denies the full implications of deafness in a subtle and usually unintentional manner. He may make inaccurate statements about the speech potentials of deaf children and the ultimate functional value of the speech that deaf persons are able to develop. Overly optimistic statements, implied or explicit, about the values of hearing aids and the effectiveness of lipreading are also expressions of denial. Euphemisms such as "He is just like any other child except that he is deaf" blur the very real differences between being prelingually deaf and having normal hearing.

Unfortunately, many who counsel parents gloss over these differences. What parents commonly encounter is the professional who fosters a denial of the implications of deafness for their child and the entire family. Because deafness is invisible, denial is easier to maintain than it is for obvious physical disabilities. For example, as a leukemic child's disease progresses, changes become so vivid that denial is almost impossible.

Parents' Mourning Period

The second phenomenon that should appear when diagnosis is confirmed is mourning. Yet, parents rarely experience fully the loss of hearing as an intense grief to be worked through psychologically (Grinker, 1969). In gestures of false kindness, professionals, physicians, and educators often help parents deny their grief over the loss. Thus, the mourning which they should experience becomes a chronically repressed grief that the parents and the deaf persons live with

> //Parents of deaf children are frequently brought to tears when discussing the deafness of fully grown sons and daughters, due to a grief which has never been fully worked through psychologically.//

indefinitely. Repression of mourning is apparent in psychological interviews with parents of deaf children who are frequently brought to tears when discussing the deafness of fully grown sons and daughters, due to a grief which has never been fully worked through psychologically.

How Denying Reality Leads to Family Stress

Breakdown in communication among family members is one of

the severest psychological stresses. The denial of the communication problems of deafness creates this kind of stress in families with deaf children. The problem grows out of the difficulties and limitations posed by lipreading and speech for persons deafened prelingually.

Why Lip-reading Is Hard

Two thirds of the 42 sounds that make up the English language are either invisible or look just like some other sound on the lips (Hardy, 1970). Furthermore, among the most difficult sounds to lipread are the most important ones, the vowels. The deaf person must grasp the few sounds that are visible in the fleeting instant they are on the lips.

Because of this ambiguity, the world's best lipreaders get about one fourth of what is said, and they are not deaf (Lowell, 1959). One reason for the poor performance of deaf persons is that in order to lipread for comprehension, the reader must have an adequate command of language; children prelingually deafened do not have it. In fact they are expected to learn language through a process which presumes that they already have language skill. As a consequence, the average deaf child gets about five percent of what is said when he must depend on lipreading (Vernon, 1970).

Achievement Levels of Deaf Students

Speech for a congenitally deaf person will never be normal, and much of it will not be intelligible. In addition to the speech problem, learning language is difficult for a deaf person because he does not hear spoken language. If he is forced to try to learn language just through lipreading, his task is almost impossible. These difficulties account for the evidence that over 30 percent of deaf students are functionally illiterate when they leave school, and only 5 percent achieve tenth-grade level. Most of the latter have only moderate hearing losses or are adventitiously deaf (McClure, 1966).

Parents do not know these facts, partly because they are not known by many who diagnose deafness. If the facts were presented, it would be painful, but it would also be reality. Until the reality of deafness is known, parent and

> //There is a huge discrepancy between parents' expectations and the child's achievements, which creates intense frustration for them both.//

child cannot cope constructively. Consequently, there is a huge discrepancy between parents' expectations and the child's achievements, which creates intense frustration for them both.

The frustration leads to an underlying stress and anger for which parents have no constructive outlets. As a result, they begin to avoid interacting with the child, and he begins to avoid interacting with them. Further attempts at child-parent communication become so stressful and frustrating that both the child and the parent understandably want to escape. Thus, the deaf child is often isolated in his own home, losing the emotional and educational benefits he needs and should get from close parental contact. The parents, in turn, lose the satisfactions of child-raising that they have a right to expect. In extreme cases, when a deaf child comes home from school for the weekend, his parents may give him some money and tell him to stay out until bedtime. More common, however, is a gradual subtle withdrawal of both parents and child.

When parents do not face the communication implications of deafness and the accompanying stress, their child does not acquire an education to match his capacity.

Deaf children have the same IQ distribution as hearing children; yet, as indicated earlier, 30 percent are functionally illiterate when they leave school (Mindel and Vernon, 1971). Sixty percent test at fifth-grade level or below. Only 5 percent of deaf students who leave school at 16 or older score as high as the tenth grade on achievement tests (McClure, 1966).

Even more tragic is the deaf child's tendency to be separated emotionally from his family. Many deaf adults are extremely bitter about their treatment by their families. They are hurt by being excluded from activities such as meal-time conversation and the planning of family activities.

HOW TOTAL COMMUNICATION BREAKS DOWN THE BARRIERS

Total Communication—the use of fingerspelling and the language of signs in conjunction with speech, lipreading, the written word, and amplification (hearing aids)—offers a reasonable approach for resolution of communication problems faced by the family with a deaf child. The addition of manual communication by fingerspelling and the language of signs in no way impedes the development of oral communication (Meadow, 1968; Vernon and Koh, 1970). Manual communication does not have the ambiguity inherent in speech and lipreading. Thus full communication between the deaf child and his parents becomes possible, which eliminates much of the stress, frustration, and anger growing out of the limitations of oral communication.

A few parents of young deaf children, upon professional advice, have begun to use both manual and oral communication simultaneously with their deaf children. While certainly not a panacea, the Total Communication approach is a step forward. In fact, its potential is so great that the National Association of the Deaf, the world's largest organization for and of deaf people, officially endorses the approach.

REFERENCES

Cholden LS: A Psychiatrist Works with Blindness. New York, American Foundation for the Blind, 1958

Grinker RG (ed): Psychiatric Diagnosis, Therapy, and Research on the Psychiatric Deaf. Final Report, Grant #RD-2407-S, Social Rehabilitation Service Department, Washington, DC, US Department of Health, Education, and Welfare, 1969

Hamburg DA: Psychological adaptive processes in life threatening injuries. Read before the Symposium on Stress, Walter Reed Medical Center, Washington, DC, 1953

Hardy M: Speechreading, in Davis H, Silverman SR (eds): Hearing and Deafness. New York, Holt, Rinehart & Winston, 1970, 335-345

Hefferman A: A psychiatric study of fifty children referred to hospital for suspected deafness, in Caplan G (ed): Emotional Problems of Childhood. New York, Basic Books, 1955, 269-292

Lowell EL: Research in speechreading: Some relationships to language development and implications for the classroom teacher. Report of Proceedings of the 39th Meeting of the Convention of American Instructors of the Deaf, 1959, 68-73

McClure WJ: Current problems and trends in the education of the deaf. Deaf American, 18: 1966, 8-14

Meadow KP: Early manual communication in relation to the deaf child's intellectual, social, and communicative function. Am Ann Deaf, 113: 29-41, 1968

Mindel ED, Vernon M: They Grow in Silence. Silver Springs, Md, National Association of the Deaf Press, 1971

Mindel ED, Vernon M: Out of the shadows and the silence. JAMA, 220: 1127-1128, 1972

Siller J: Psychological situation of the disabled with spinal cord injuries. Rehab Lit, 30: 290-296, 1969

Vernon M: Potential, achievement, and rehabilitation in the deaf population. Rehab Lit, 31: 258-267, 1970

Vernon M: Mind over mouth: A rationale for total communication. Volta Review, 74, 1972, 529-540

Vernon M, Koh SD: Early manual communication and deaf children's achievement. Am Ann Deaf, 115: 527-536, 1970

Part III:
THE EDUCATION OF DEAF CHILDREN

The authors guide parents through the mazes of formal education and tell how, where, and when communication begins.

Schools for Deaf Children
•
DAVID M. DENTON, RICHARD G. BRILL, MARGARET S. KENT and NANCY M. SWAIKO

WHEN THE WORLD IS SILENT: WHAT DEAFNESS MEANS

Everyone understands that effective educational methods must be flexible to accomodate the specific needs of students. Therefore, before setting forth the objectives of education for deaf children, it is necessary to consider deafness and its implications for the deaf child as they relate to his specific needs.

Deafness is a unique handicap that is not visible physically and is confined to only a small part of the anatomy. Yet its consequences are phenomenal with regard to the emotional, social, and educational growth of the deaf child.

The largest part of man's learning is acquired through hearing. It is the channel through which an abundance of stimuli trigger the individual's behavior, simple to complex. As Fusfield (1967) writes, "Hearing is the basic scanning, alerting, and contact sense in man. When deafness ensues, the individual is deprived of his basic sense for environmental contact and exploration." His sense of hearing is what keeps man in constant touch with his environment. Even more important is the vital role of hearing in human communication and interaction. The ability to communicate is one of man's most precious gifts. The silent world of the deaf individual—the isolation of a person unable to make free and normal contact with other human beings—can be a tremendous barrier to his full participation in life.

Deafness is a sensory handicap which denies the individual the vital stimulus of sound and the spoken word. At best, we who hear can only talk about deafness. If we were to let others know what deafness is like from actual experience, we would reiterate the immense social isolation imposed upon the individual by the absence of hearing. This point is well portrayed in Greenberg's book, <u>In This Sign</u>. Her realistic account of Janice and Abel's life in a hearing world conveys to the reader a deep insight into the terrors and isolation resulting from an inability to communicate.

WHEN EDUCATION OF DEAF CHILDREN BEGAN

Formal education of deaf children in the United States began with the efforts of Thomas Hopkins Gallaudet, who was graduated from Yale in 1805 at the age of eighteen. Gallaudet planned to enter the ministry, but because of ill health he remained at his home in Hartford, Connecticut. During this time he became interested in the education of deaf children when he undertook the task of teaching Alice Cogswell, the deaf daughter of a neighbor.

During the same period from 1805 to 1815, John Braidwood, son of Thomas Braidwood, a leading lipreading instructor in England, was establishing a school for deaf children in Virginia. Thomas Gallaudet went to England in 1817 to learn the Braidwood method of instruction. The Braidwoods, however, did not wish Gallaudet to learn their method only to return to America and open a school that would compete with John Braidwood's in Virginia. Instead, they offered Gallaudet a staff position in their school. Gallaudet then heard l'abbé Sicard, who was in charge of Charles De l'Epée's manual school for deaf children in Paris, lecture in London, and told him of his wish to educate deaf children. Sicard persuaded Gallaudet to attend his school in Paris and learn the language of signs and fingerspelling. With Gallaudet's decision to go to the Paris school, the future of many American deaf children was determined, for Sicard was an advocate of the manual method, while the Braidwoods taught only the oral.

At the Sicard school, Gallaudet became a friend of Laurent Clerc, a deaf teacher. He told Clerc of the great need for teachers of deaf children in America, and after approximately two months of training, he and Clerc left France for America to open a school in Hartford.

Four years later, the school had made such excellent progress that it received federal subsidization and was established as The American Asylum for the Deaf, now known as The American School for the Deaf, in Hartford, Connecticut.

Other schools for deaf children were established in the United States, but not all of them adopted the manual approach in spite of its spectacular success. Reports, however, began to show the success of the oral method as it was taught in England and Germany. In 1843 Horace Mann returned from Europe with favorable and enthusiastic reports on the oral approach, but advocates of the manual method did not weaken, and speech and lipreading were taught only in the smallest private schools. However, in 1867, the philanthropist John Clarke donated 550,000 dollars to help establish an oral school for deaf children in Northampton, Massachusetts.

By 1900, there were 57 public residential schools

and various programs for deaf children in this country.

PRESENT EDUCATIONAL ADMINISTRATION: PUBLIC AND PRIVATE

The flux in day-school development stems from the need to accomodate hard-of-hearing children.

Since one half of the deaf children in the United States attend public residential schools, it is important to note their various types of governing bodies:

State Board of Education
Specially appointed boards
(Board of Trustees or Board of Directors)
State Department of Public Instruction
State Board of Regents
Department of Public Welfare
State Board of Health
State Department of Child and Family Services
State Board of Control
Department of Mental Health and Corrections
Department of Institutions

The administrative structure of public residential schools varies from state to state.

Sixteen of the 66 residential schools were established as private schools, but are classified now as public residential schools because most of their financial support comes from the state. In some instances, the state pays a flat tuition for each child enrolled, and in others the state reimburses the school for its operating costs at the end of the fiscal year.

With the exception of Gallaudet College, privately established schools which receive public support admit within a given geographical area all children who meet their criteria. No charge is made for board, room, laundry, tuition, or minor medical care.

A program that may serve well in one state may not be adaptable to another because of differences in area, total population, pattern of urban and rural developments, and legal and financial structures of the state and local school systems. However, on the whole, deaf children of many states would benefit as a result of cooperative planning and policymaking, and it is hoped that many more cooperative plans will develop.

WHAT CHILDREN LEARN: HOW PARENTS CAN FIND OUT

One of the basic aims of educators of deaf children is to develop the child's competence in communication skills, in order to better enable him to engage in meaningful human interaction. Communication is but a tool which grows out of significant human encounter and life experiences. Thus, the term educator can be applied not only to teachers in the child's school environment, but to parents, siblings, relatives, friends, and all who come in contact with him.

Lanugage is the core of the deaf child's education. Language is based upon and grows out of communication. Communication is an act of participation in life that cannot be specifically taught. Instead, the child must be provided opportunities to interact with others, and he must be given the necessary communication tools to express himself. These serve as the initial implements for linguistic interaction and intellectual growth. Equally important, a child uses these basic tools to discover and explore his environment. Out of his meaningful discoveries and human interaction emerges self-discovery of and the unique development of his individual personality. Communication is the beginning of understanding.

Members of the medical profession are usually the first professionals who advise parents about their child's future welfare. These professionals should therefore be informed of the medical and educational aspects of deafness, and more importantly, they should be aware of how "the condition of deafness interfers with the normal progression of the child's language and psychosocial development (Brill, 1970). Professionals should also be prepared and willing to help parents express their first reactions to the diagnosis of their child's deafness; that is, "the need to discuss, ventilate and understand their feelings toward their deaf child" (Brill, 1970).

The first step forward in educating the deaf child is taken when parents and educators accept the reality and irreversibility of deafness. By understanding the full implications of deafness we can best meet the total needs of the child.

The next step is to sidestep the manual-oral controversy and then consider whether the child should enroll in a residential school or a day school; both have partisan support.

Day School or Residential School?

Day schools are geared more to meet the oral communication needs of hard-of-hearing children and to help them prepare for integration into classrooms with normal hearing children.

For many profoundly deaf children of hearing parents, residential schools which practice manual communication offer the child the environment of constant communication often lacking in the home.

One disadvantage of residential schools is that school life cannot replace home life with family members. Realizing this, most residential schools make efforts for their children to return home as often as possible, frequently every weekend.

Every school and its program varies, as does every child. When a family has the choice of sending a child to a day-school program or a public residential school, they should visit both to have the child evaluated at each. In this way, family and counselors may be able to determine what the best program is for a particular child at a particular time. When parents visit, they must be sure to ask to see programs for the oldest children as well as for the youngest. This will give them a better picture of what their child will eventually achieve. Parents should also observe classes of slower children even though they may be sure their own child is one of the smartest. By doing so, they may be assured that they are not observing only the most able children, who may hardly be characteristic of the school population.

METHODS OF COMMUNICATION: WHEN TO USE WHICH

For the past hundred years there has been a deep and emotional conflict, commonly referred to as the oral-manual controversy, over what methods of communication ought to be used in educating the deaf child. Many proponents of early education of deaf infants believe, for example that the simultaneous method should be started in the cradle and not postponed to the secondary school years.

SYSTEMS OF COMMUNICATION METHODS

The Rochester Method—Established by Westervelt at the Rochester School for the Deaf nearly 100 years ago as an attempt to overcome the objection to the syntactical deficiencies of American Sign Language. The Rochester Method utilized the manual alphabet and speech simultaneously. Each word is fingerspelled in English syntax as it is spoken. Proponents of this method are opposed to signing, which they feel cheats deaf children of language-learning opportunities. They emphasize the point that deaf children must see English to learn English.

Oral Method—Refers to expressive communication through speech and receptive communication through speechreading. In most educational programs, the term pure oral describes a system which does not allow manual communication of any kind. Reading and writing are included as legitimate means of communication in the oral system, along with speech and speechreading.

Simultaneous Method—Another long established form of communication which adds speech to any form of sign language. This is used extensively at Gallaudet College where students with manual and oral educational backgrounds receive instruction in the same classroom. By adding spoken language, the manual presentation hopefully follows more acceptable English word order. The simultaneous method has been practiced in the upper classes of residential schools for many years (Kent, 1972). Many proponents of early education of deaf infants believe, for example, that the simultaneous method should be started in the cradle and not postponed to the secondary school years.

Total Communication—Contrary to what some people think, not just another name for the simultaneous method. The difference lies in the philosophical point of view embodied in the concept. Total Communication recognizes the needs of all deaf children. It takes into account the fact that learning to communicate proceeds in a hierarchy, beginning with the most primitive and progressing to the more complex and sophisticated use of symbol systems that involve all sensory modalities, visual and auditory. Each child learns according to his needs and capabilities. Proponents place special emphasis on involving both family and school to provide a consistent and stimulating environment in which all deaf children can thrive and prosper. Total Communication uses the language of signs, fingerspelling, amplification of residual hearing (hearing aids), speech, speechreading, and the written word, all at once.

Recently Developed Sign Systems—Four similar but somewhat varying forms. They are Manual English, Signed English, Visual English, and SEE (Seeing Essential English). All are based on the American Sign Language and employ word order or syntax of the English language. Signed English uses signs and fingerspelling according to basic English syntax. Manual English and SEE add morphemes, or word parts, which have meaning, such as word endings, verb tenses, prefixes, and suffixes. Visual English is a linguistically based system using American Sign Language vocabulary plus a more elaborate vocabulary of morphemes, which take on new meanings according to their context (Kent, 1972).

The fundamental difference in the methods controversy is the question of the legitimacy of the use of manual communication with or without oral communication with the deaf child.

Pros and Cons in the Oral-Manual Controversy

"The fundamental position of the oralist is that training in speech and speech reading gives an easier adjustment to the world in which speech is the chief medium of communication" (Davis, 1947). Confirmed oralists believe that every deaf child of normal intelligence must be motivated to use speech and speechreading constantly and solely. They feel that any use of manual communication interferes with the acquisition of speech.

To the naive and hearing observer, the fundamental problem associated with deafness appears to be an inability to speak, but such an observer lacks the awareness that the fundamental problem is lack of the ability to hear language. Just learning speech itself does not teach language. Hearing parents often initially support programs claiming to be able to teach their deaf child to talk and lipread so that he can be just like everyone else.

Unfortunately, many profoundly deaf children fail to communicate orally because their profound hearing loss even with high amplification does not permit them to receive enough sound or speech clues to develop adequate speech and speechreading skills spontaneously. It is unrealistic to expect a remnant of residual hearing to support spontaneous growth in language upon exposure to a totally oral environment.

What Hearing Aids Do

The role of amplification in the growth and development of

language is highly dependent on both the qualitative and quantitative aspects of the hearing impairment as well as the amplification system. Thus a child learns in spite of the distortions or limitations of his own auditory system plus those inherent in the hearing aid or amplification system employed in the classroom. The result is a phenomenon often overlooked: these distortions and limitations become magnified when they are amplified and may very well make it more difficult for a student to associate an auditory signal with the spoken or written language. Hence the quality of audition is a vital factor in assessing the extent to which a given child may rely on amplification to support language growth.

The position of the person who supports Total Communication is summed up in the phrase, fitting the method to the child rather than the child to the method.

Total Communication

Very young deaf children rely heavily on nonverbal communication. There is a certain naturalness of gesture in the normal learning process which mediates and enriches language learning for a child. With knowledge of American Sign Language, which includes signs, fingerspelling, and relies heavily on facial expression and body movement, parents can engage in meaningful communication with their deaf child at an early age.

Signs can play a vital role in establishing language for the very young deaf child by providing a medium for him to acquire the language experiences from which he can generate his own language rules or syntax. Adults enhance his progress when they use signs along with speech in their daily contact with him. The adults reflect the child's ideas in the give and take of conversation. Units of meaningful communication expand from single words, to phrases, to sentences. One linguist refers to this process as the "maternal reflective method of language

> //A deaf child learns language best at an early age in a natural setting, preferably in the home, through a meaningful exchange of ideas with someone he loves.//

teaching of the deaf child (Van Uden, 1968). Realistically, a young deaf child never learns enough language in the classroom. "He learns it best at an early age in a natural setting, preferably in the home, through meaningful exchange of ideas with someone he loves. We believe signs play a vital role in this process" (Kent, 1970).

Our endorsement of any symbol system for communication would have to include one that is accessible to the very young deaf child, so that he can manipulate the symbols for himself to abstract his own meanings and generate his own language rules. The child would progress naturally from the simplest to more complex forms. We would also expect the symbol system to be one which both school and home would employ consistently to culminate in a general mastery of English syntax at an appropriate age of seven or eight. Lenneberg (1970) states, "Normal children can repeat correctly only that which is formed by rules they have already mastered. This is the best indication that language does not come about by simple imitation but that the child abstracts regularities or relations from the language he hears (uses) which he then applies to build up language for himself as an apparatus of principles." Hopefully, acquisition of a reliable visual symbol system would do much to liberate the deaf child from the bondage of dependency on programmed language in the classroom, which gives rise to artificial language expression and sterility of thought which are almost impossible to overcome.

A deaf child can only learn to communicate under the same conditions as a hearing child. He must be free to interact and experiment with a reliable symbol system, find out how it works, continue to use and expand it through practice. This process promotes optimum language growth in accordance with the child's intellectual potential.

What must be remembered is that neither method of communication, oral or manual, is right or wrong. Instead, we hope everyone realizes that the child's priorities must come first when evaluating the effectiveness or limitations of a method. We encourage learning by residual hearing through amplification to its fullest potential, but above all, we respect the right of the profoundly deaf child to have the opportunity to learn to communicate with a reliable visual symbol system.

LEVELS OF EDUCATION

The Preschool Years

The preschool years are the most crucial period psychologically, educationally, and linguistically in the life of the deaf child and his family. Parents play a vital role in determining the outcome of these critical and most receptive years before their child enters school.

The most critical decision parents may ever make is choosing to learn a reliable visual symbol system to use with their very young deaf child. Research shows that early manual communication enhances the child's ability to eventually attain speech and speechreading and greatly increases his level of language and educational achievement. Thus, early childhood education should emphasize manual as well as oral communication to give all deaf children this great advantage.

The home should be a stimulating language environment for the deaf child, just as it is for the hearing child. The child must be exposed to and given the opportunity to experiment with visual symbols that will make it possible for him to acquire language.

The deaf parent of a deaf child easily establishes communication by using the language of signs. Hearing parents face a much greater challenge because they must learn a new, visual mode of communication. But when resourceful parents respond naturally to whatever gestures the young child may initiate to indicate his needs, both the child and the parents are on their way to communicating. It is the mother, primarily, who sets the stage for this first important step in communication.

How Manual Communication Evolves

A gesture system, or "baby talk," may easily evolve into a more sophisticated language system when hearing parents learn manual communication. If they are fortunate enough to observe how deaf parents communicate so naturally with their deaf children, hearing parents can learn to provide the same, reliable, unambigious visual system so necessary for the spontaneous growth of communication and language. Classes in the language of signs are becoming available in many communities through adult education courses in community colleges, university clinics, and in high schools. It is important that hearing parents of profoundly deaf children learn to be reasonably proficient in manual communication as early as possible.

When parents successfully meet the challenge of communication, many satisfying experiences occur. They can enjoy their deaf child. The child begins to blossom in a warm, accepting, and stimulating language environment. He becomes an active, participating member of the family. He is spared the monotony of meaningless drill. When it is time to learn to read and write and to take on the intricacies of speech lessons and academics, he is ready and eager to transfer trust in his parents to trust in his teachers.

In order for their young, profoundly deaf child to acquire language in the preschool years, parents must (Kent, 1973):

* seek a reliable diagnosis at the earliest possible date to

understand their child's hearing impairment.
* understand the degree of their child's hearing loss and the extent to which amplification may or may not contribute to communication and language acquisition.
* learn to communicate proficiently in the language of signs.
* appreciate how all children acquire language so that they may facilitate language growth for their own child: that there is a critical timetable for learning language; that signs can become the first language for the profoundly deaf child; that signs can facilitate speech and speechreading skills; and the profoundly deaf child can achieve language competence early in life if he lives in a stimulating language environment.
* bear the ultimate responsibility for decisions which affect their child's progress.

When It's Time for School

The trend in most schools for deaf children is to admit them at the pre-primary age and educate them through the secondary level. Many schools group and regroup the children according to their language ability primarily. This nongraded developmental program more nearly answers the needs of the students and reduces problems a child may encounter when he compares himself to his hearing peers. A child who feels seriously retarded academically becomes frustrated.

The school's first obligation is to prepare the child academically, so he can go farther in any direction he chooses, be it academic or vocational, and to orient him for effective functioning later on in his life. People fail not because they

//People fail not because they lack skills, generally, but because they are unable to communicate effectively.//

lack skills, generally, but because they are unable to communicate effectively.

Language Development—The Vital Component

==Language is any symbol system used for the exchange of thoughts, ideas, and feelings between two individuals.==

Analysis of records in the Maryland School for the Deaf shows that 9 in 10 deaf children are born so today, in contrast to 5 in 10 more than 30 years ago. This means that most of today's deaf students never had the opportunity to acquire language normally. Myklebust (1956) divides language into three categories: inner, receptive and expressive.

> Inner language is the symbol system used for thinking, memory, and imagination, reasoning, or talking to ourselves. Receptive language is the symbol system used to comprehend the ideas of others. Expressive language is the symbol system used to communicate ideas to someone other than ourselves. The hearing infant is exposed to spoken language for about eight months before he begins to comprehend what is being said. An association must be made between experience and the symbol being used for it. When that association is accomplished, inner language is established, and it is only then that receptive language can begin. From about the ninth month to about one year, the inner and receptive language develop simultaneously to the point that expressive language is possible. This means that at about twelve to thirteen months of age the hearing child speaks his first word. The genetic sequence followed is inner language first, receptive language second, and expressive

language third. This genetic basis for language
can be used as a frame of reference for all
children, hearing or deaf.

The child learns language by manipulating its
symbols and by actively coping with his environment.

//Postponing language acquisition until
the child begins formal education at
age 4, 5, or 6 places a burden of
frustration on him that too often
seriously retards his educational
achievement.//

There is a critical time for learning language for the deaf
child, just as there is for the hearing child. Postponing
language acquisition until the child begins formal education
at age 4, 5, or 6 places a burden of frustration on him that
too often seriously retards his educational achievement. The
deaf child has the right to the same opportunity to learn to
communicate as his hearing peers.

Because signs are so graphic and easily manipulated,
the very young deaf child can freely experiment with them,
as his "coin of exchange." Only through such free
experimentation can a young child discover and generalize
meaning for himself. To reverse the process—to force the
child to abstract meaning solely from adult initiated language—is
to deprive him of self-discovery and interferes with and often
retards his cognitive growth.

What Total Communication Accomplishes

Total Communication is a multi-leveled approach to the
education of deaf children. It implies the right of the deaf
child to have all forms of communication available in order

that he may develop the dual goals of language competence and scholastic success. This means introducing a reliable, receptive and expressive symbol system in the preschool years, between the ages of 1 and 5. Total Communication includes all language modalities: child-devised gestures, the formal language of signs, speech, speechreading, fingerspelling, amplification of residual hearing (hearing aids) reading and writing.

To rely on speechreading as a receptive channel for learning a new language on the assumption that manual communication inhibits oral skills means there is no awareness of individual differences in deaf children or their emotional problems arising from frustrations to communicate. Dr. Richard G. Brill, Superintendent of the California School for the Deaf, Riverside, states (1970):

> The evidence seems quite clear that total communication is what is needed for all deaf people from the youngest years to the oldest. Communication is the person's ability to use his language for expressing ideas, needs, and feelings. As Meadow points out, a four-year-old hearing child not only has the vocabulary of from 2,000 to 3,000 words, but in addition, he follows the rules of grammar and syntax that enable him to combine these words in many meaningful ways. The typical deaf child of the same age with exclusively oral communication has only a few words and rarely expands these words into expressions for additional meanings.

As Ms. Lee Katz, past president of the International Associations of Parents of the Deaf says, "Total Communication begins in the home." Schools, such as the Maryland School for the Deaf, employ Total Communication beginning with parent counseling when the child is around 2, involving the whole family. The counseling teams go into the home to teach communication skills to parents, show them how to use total communication, and how to make efficient use of the child's individual hearing aid.

While one member of a parent-counseling team works with the parents, another helps the child. There is a constant exchange of information between the counselors and the parents, and each week there is an assessment of progress. The primary objective of the program is to establish communication between the parents and the child and to get language started in the home. A more positive and realistic acceptance of the child's handicap is possible as the family is able to establish communication with him. Parents in this program also become involved with parents of other deaf children thus finding they are not alone.

The child whose family takes advantage of the parent-counseling program can expect greater success when he eventually enters school. He is ready, just as the hearing child, for what education has to offer. Too many others without this service must wait until school age before he begins to learn to develop any language skills.

Total Communication enables the children to use every possible means of communication to learn, to understand, to exchange thoughts, feelings and ideas. Total Communication gives the child freedom to develop his intellectual capacities without restraints beyond those already imposed by his handicap.

In schools where Total Communication is practiced, there is open and free interaction among children and houseparents, teachers, and administrators. It is the school's contention that no one learns language by learning grammar; that language involves individuals, not charts; and that a child-adult and child-child interaction is what develops language. In "Psycholinguistics and Deafness" (1970), Dr. Donald Moores writes
> Language learning is not such a passive process as had been assumed. A child learns his

language by interacting with it, by actively coping with and manipulating his environment. He does this on the basis of unsystematic, usually unplanned language input. It appears that the child develops his language through a number of successive, increasingly complex stages, and it is possible that the structures at the earliest most primitive levels are similar for all children, no matter what language their parents speak.

Hierarchy of Communication for the Congenitally Deaf Child

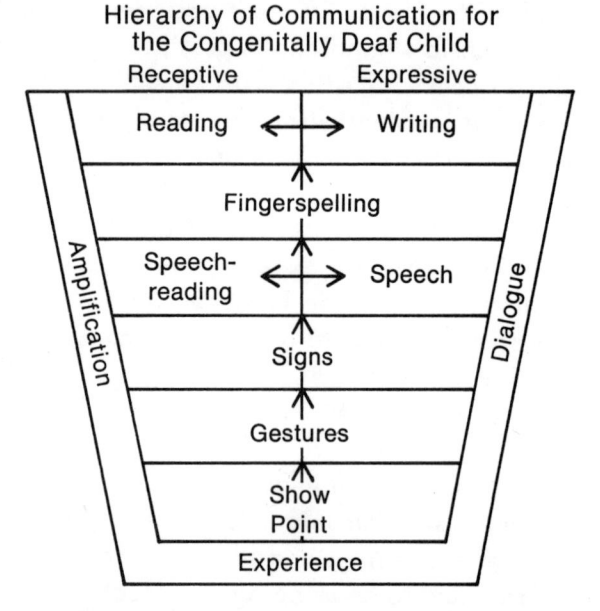

Receptive — Expressive

Reading ↔ Writing
Fingerspelling
Speech-reading ↔ Speech
Signs
Gestures
Show Point
Experience

Amplification — Dialogue

FIGURE 1 Hierarchy of communication for the congenitally deaf child.

LEARNING SIGNS STEP-BY-STEP

Self-Initiated Gestures

In the initial interview with parents of a very young deaf child, the counselor routinely asks how he communicates. The mother usually replies that the child takes her by the hand to show her what he wants or points to the milk in the refrigerator when he wants a drink. We label this gesture point and show, as the most elementary attempt by the child to ask for something. The resourceful child soon invents some obvious gestures for sleeping, eating or going to bed. When encouraged, many deaf children develop an elaborate gesture system understood within the family. The adult deaf individual refers to these gestures as "home signs," recognizing that their own deaf children go through this developmental state too. It is important to note that the meaning of these signs is clear to the child since they are self-initiated and not superimposed by an adult. For this reason we view individual gesture systems as an important manifestation of the ability to symbolize. These primitive gestures evolve naturally into a more formal language of signs when signs are encouraged and used with the child.

Speech Associated With Signs

The next step is to associate speech and speechreading with signs. When the adult speaks as he signs, the child soon attempts to say the word along with the signs, too, and before long he can respond to speechreading in the same manner. This is learning by conditioning, the simplest, most effective way of learning. We have noted that a child finds it easier to respond to speechreading after he makes speech attempts. The profoundly deaf child does not have to wait until he is four or five for this to occur. The deaf child of deaf parents begins this process at the same age the hearing child, between the ages of one and two.

As we understand the effects of total communication more clearly, we can refine and document them.

OBSERVED EFFECTS OF TOTAL COMMUNICATION

1. Signs are the easiest means of getting the very young congenitally deaf child to communicate in the true sense of the word, that is, to express his own ideas. When this happens, we see positive changes in behavior and improvement in interpersonal relationships. The deaf child joins the family as a fully participating member.
2. Signs reinforce speechreading and audition when the adult (teacher, parent, houseparent) signs and talks simultaneously, and the child has amplification adequate for his needs. For the child who cannot benefit from amplification, signs reinforce speechreading. Speech for this child must be developed purely on a kinesthetic basis. Language development, however, is not tied to his progress in speech.
3. When speech and signs are practiced simultaneously, acceptable syntax is more apt to occur. This is usually the way the hearing person learns to associate signs with words. The combination of speech and signs provides a syntactic model for the deaf child to imitate, both visually and aurally.
4. Audition (high-gain amplification) reinforces aural-oral skills (speech and speechreading) for many deaf children when the equipment is of a quality to reach the hearing impairment. Success depends upon auditory feedback or the degree to which the child can hear his own speech as well as the speech of others.
5. Fingerspelling reinforces reading and writing and requires a similar level of maturation and background of language experience as reading and writing. It is no more practical to start the preschool deaf child with fingerspelling

> than to start the hearing preschool child's language development with reading and writing. Signs provide "the coin of exchange" for transmission of ideas and for the eventual generation of syntax at an early age.

Total Communication as an inclusive system and not an arbitrary nor exclusive method. In the system of Total Communication, meaningful choices and decisions are made by the child rather than the teacher. Total Communication embraces all the different components of communication. So, as Denton said before a recent symposium on communication,

> "If you want to discuss speechreading, then that is a part of Total Communication. If you want to discuss auditory training, fine; that is also a part of Total Communication. If you want to consider the early attempts at self-expression of an infant, manifested through gestures, then that is a part of Total Communication. Or, if you want to talk about speech development and the language of signs, they are parts of the system also. The deaf child is offered the whole package and thereby has the opportunity to screen out that which he can use and that which is appropriate to his particular developmental level. Using such a system, a deaf child has the opportunity to generate and to develop his own language rules the way we do. These rules, of course evolve through language experience.

The promotion of a system of total communication for deaf children is also based upon the obvious reality that children simply can never learn enough language in the classroom. They must learn it in the hallway, in the alley, in the dormitory, but, most importantly, in the home" (Denton, 1970a).

HOW TEACHING METHODS DIFFER FOR TEACHERS OF DEAF CHILDREN

Since lack of language is the deaf child's most important handicap, every teacher of deaf children must have sufficient course work and practice teaching with deaf children, and to understand how most effectively to teach language to them. For speech and speechreading, the ideal teacher should have excellent speech in order to demonstrate articulate speech formation to the children. Normal hearing is essential to analyze the articulation of each child's speech.

Oral schools which forbid manual communication obviously would not employ a deaf teacher because he might find it difficult to teach speech. Most deaf persons who are teachers are employed in residential schools using manual communication as part of their educational procedures. Even though a hearing teacher may be outstanding in manual communication skills, he has limitations, because the language of signs is a second language for him. For the deaf person though, who lost his hearing prelingually or who used manual communication most of his life, it is his native language. Because of their native fluency with the language of signs deaf people are often better able to understand the manual communication of deaf children. In addition, because most deaf people have had the same institutional educational experiences, deaf teachers have more insight into the problems confronted by the deaf child as he grows. In the school situation, the deaf teacher can be a source of inspiration to the children, someone they identify with and to whom they can easily relate. Deaf teachers,

//The deaf teacher can be a source of inspiration to the children, someone they identify with and to whom they can easily relate.//

because of their life experiences, have a realistic grasp and understanding of the problems resulting from the deaf child's poor understanding of language. Qualified deaf teachers also have great potential for guidance counseling, perhaps even more than equally qualified hearing teachers.

State Certification Required for Teachers of Deaf Children

Students in training to teach deaf children do most of their work in graduate school. The trend today is to train teachers within specialized areas, such as preschool, elementary school, and secondary school. Preparing teachers of deaf children involves specialized study over and above a prospective teacher's basic general education. Therefore, states require certificates of licensure and credentials for teachers of deaf children.

Studies show that states differ greatly in their certification and licensure requirements. With so many separate states issuing certificates and licenses and changing their requirements from time to time, it is not practical to summarize certification standards for the various states.

REFERENCES

Brill RG: Total communication as a basis of educating prelingually deaf children. Frederick, Maryland, Communication Symposium, 8-12, 1970

Brill RG: <u>Administrative and Professional Developments in the Education of the Deaf</u>. Washington, DC, Gallaudet College Press, 1971

Communication Symposium, The Maryland School for the Deaf, 1970

Davis H: <u>Hearing and Deafness</u>. New York, Rinehart, 1947

Davis H, Silverman SR, et al: <u>Hearing and Deafness</u> (Rev ed). New York, Holt, Rinehart & Winston, 1960

Denton DM: To the profession. Frederick, Maryland, Proceedings of the Teacher Institute, 1969, 2-7

Denton DM: Remarks in support of a system of total communication. Frederick, Maryland, Communication Symposium, 1970, 5-7

Denton DM: <u>Total Communication</u>. Maryland School for the Deaf, 1970

Denton DM: Educational crises. Paper presented to the TRIPOD Conference, Memphis, Tennessee, 1971

Denton DM: A philosophical foundation for Total
   Communication. Address given at the Indiana School
   for the Deaf's Preschool Parents, 1972

Denton DM: Remarks at the Regional Conference on the
   Coordination of Rehabilitation and Educational Services
   for the Deaf, 1972

Fusfield IS: A Handbook of Readings in Education of the
   Deaf and Post School Implications. Springfield,
   Illinois, Charles C Thomas, 1967

Greenberg J: In This Sign. New York, Holt, Rinehart &
   Winston, 1970

Kent MS: Are signs legitimate? Am Ann Deaf 115: 497-498,
   1970

Kent MS: Total communication at the Maryland school
   for the deaf. Deaf Am 23: 5-8, 1971

Kent MS: Language growth and development of the deaf
   child. Paper presented at the in-service workshop,
   Carver School for the Deaf, Annapolis, Maryland.
   Md Bull 91, 1971

Kent MS: Signs—what system? Md Bull 102: 93, 94, 1972

Kent MS: Statements on the Maryland school for the deaf. Paper presented at a Statewide Symposium, 1972

Kent MS: Bridge over troubled waters: Parents must communicate. Paper presented at Council of Organizations Serving the Deaf Forum, Williamsburg, Virginia, 1973 (To be published in Proceedings of Council of Organizations Serving the Deaf, Williamsburg, Virginia, 1973)

Lenneberg EH: On explaining language. In Lehmen J (ed): Selected Readings in Language for Teachers of the Hearing Impaired. New York, Simon and Schuster, 1970

Meadow K: Early manual communication in relation to the deaf child's intellectual, social and communicative functioning. Am Ann Deaf 113: 29-41, 1968

Mindel E, Vernon M: They Grow in Silence. Silver Springs, Md, The National Association of the Deaf Press, 1971

Moores D: Psycholinguistics and deafness. Am Ann Deaf 115: 37-48, 1970

Myklebust HR: Language disorders in children. Except Child 22: 164, 1956

Myklebust HR: The Psychology of Deafness. New York, Grune & Stratton, 1967

Proceedings of the Teacher Institute, Maryland School for the Deaf, 1969

Van Uden A: <u>A World of Language for Deaf Children</u>. St. Michielsgestel, The Netherlands, 1968

Why, despite a long history of formal education for deaf people in the US, do so many remain uneducated? Total Communication may help educate more.

Total Communication as a Basis of Educating Deaf Children*

RICHARD G. BRILL

PROGRESS RECORD FOR EDUCATION OF DEAF PEOPLE

The education of the deaf is the oldest form of special education in the United States. The first permanent school for deaf students was established in Hartford, Connecticut, in 1817. The education of blind children and the education of mentally retarded children followed many years later. We have much to be proud of in the more than 150 years that we have been educating the deaf, but we also have much to be concerned about. No professional educator that I know of is particularly proud of the general level of education obtained by the huge majority of deaf students. No professional educator is satisfied with the communication skills of the huge majority of deaf students. We all seek something better.

Perhaps much of the lack of progress is due to what is sometimes referred to as the One Hundred Years War or the

*From an address at a Communication Symposium, Maryland School for the Deaf, March 13, 1970, and reprinted in the West Virginia Tablet, February, 1971. Published by permission.

tremendous controversy in regard to methods of communication in educating deaf children. The two first entirely oral schools for deaf children were established in 1867, so we can pinpoint with great accuracy the time the "war of methods" began.

This One Hundred Years War has been characterized by emotion on the part of both educators and parents, by lack of precise thinking, including the understanding of terminology and definition of terms, and finally by lack of perspective in regard to the appropriate relationships between means and ends.

We will describe the deaf child and define some terms used in the field. We will then proceed to place the problems in perspective by considering our general objectives. Next, we will consider certain long-held assumptions. Finally, we will present positive reasons for using Total Communication with deaf children, starting with their preschool years and continuing through their entire school program.

THE QUALITY OF DEAFNESS DETERMINES THE EDUCATIONAL METHOD

As our major concern is the education of deaf children, the most important word to define is deafness or deaf. Simply stated, a person is deaf who cannot hear and understand connected speech, though such a person may, and generally does, have extensive sound perception. He can hear many sounds when they are amplified sufficiently and he may be able to hear individual speech sounds, but he does not hear enough of them to be able to understand connected speech. In contrast, the hard-of-hearing person has a hearing loss, but can understand connected speech with or without

> //If a child can understand someone else's speech through his hearing alone—even though amplified—he is hard-of-hearing, not deaf.//

amplification. A very simple test to differentiate between the two is to have the individual close his eyes. If he can understand someone else's speech through his hearing alone—even though amplified—he is hard-of-hearing.

Distinguishing Prelingually and Postlingually Deaf Children

For educational purposes, we make a very important distinction between those who are prelingually deaf and those who are postlingually deaf. The prelingually deaf child was born deaf or became deaf at such an early age that he never had an opportunity to learn language and to learn speech through his hearing. In contrast, the postlingually deaf child had relatively normal hearing the first two or three years of life at least, so that he was able to learn language and speech as other children do. For educational purposes, the distinction between the two is tremendous.

In addition, I would like to add another category that we might call the pseudo-hard-of-hearing. One definition of pseudo is a deceptive resemblance to a specific thing. This applies to the child who has a great amount of residual hearing. However, he does not have enough to really learn language and speech through his hearing alone, even when highly amplified, except through quite structured lessons from a qualified teacher. Some children fall into this category because even though they know and understand a great deal of language through hearing with amplification, they have very great difficulty in understanding any language or any subject they have not dealt with before.

It is important to note that the huge majority of children enrolled in most schools for deaf students today are prelingually deaf. The postlingually deaf child is really rather rare because the advances in modern medicine prevent all but a very few children from becoming deaf as a result of the high fever accompanying the typical childhood diseases of measles, mumps, whooping cough, etc. In the California School for the Deaf, where we have 580 children enrolled, 95 percent are prelingually deaf. We have two children in the entire school who can be identified as postlingually deaf, and we have about 35 children who are hard of hearing. In general, hard-of-hearing children should not be educated with deaf children because the basic educational problem is different, and there are many kinds of situations that are neither beneficial to the deaf children nor to the hard-of-hearing children when both are attending the same school. However, as a practical matter, there are situations where even though the ideal solution to the hard-of-hearing child's problem is not a school for the deaf, it is the only practical one because there is no other school or agency meeting his needs.

Precise Definition of Hearing Loss

Within recent years the term hearing impaired has become prevalent in certain educational areas. The term is global in that it must include the prelingually deaf, the postlingually deaf, the hard-of-hearing child at the very least, and, possibly, the aphasic. It is difficult to see how using such a global and imprecise term can help clarify the objectives and responsibilities of a school that has as its primary mission the education of deaf children. We not infrequently have instances of some parents who, for one reason or another, refuse to refer to the child as a deaf child, but always refer to him as a hard-of-hearing child—in spite of the fact that the child cannot hear and understand speech through the ear, as evidenced by the fact that he has never learned language through hearing. Perhaps because of guilt feelings on the part of the parent or his inability to accept the child's handicap, he uses this euphemism when he insists on referring to the child as hard-of-hearing rather than deaf. One wonders whether some educators may not have equally invalid reasons for insisting that programs always be referred to as for the hearing impaired, as though this made the whole program much more modern, rather than using the term deaf, which can have objective specificity. The use of the term <u>hearing impaired</u> primarily confuses the issue as for as appropriate educational procedures are concerned.

How Education for the Deaf Child Differs

What are our objectives in educating deaf children? It may be assumed that they are essentially the same as those we have for the education of hearing children. These have been frequently cited as the achievement of self-realization, the development of proper human relationships, the attainment of economic efficiency, and the assumption of civic responsibility. Put in another way, this means that each individual must learn to live with himself; he must learn to live with other people; he must attain a particular level of economic efficiency in order to support himself and contribute to society; and he should assume civic responsibility within the community of which he is a member.

Education of deaf children differs from the education of other children, even though we have the same objectives, because the teaching of deaf children is complicated by the fact that they do not have normal communication skills. This, in turn, affects their social, psychological and emotional development, as well as their general educational achievement.

COMMUNICATION: THE CORE OF THE PROBLEM

Because deafness creates a communication handicap, it is the responsibility of the school to teach communication in all its phases: language, speech, speechreading, reading, and writing. I would add manual communication also. Communication is but a tool. It is the school's responsibility to teach all the subject matter and content material possible in the time available. The school also has the responsibility of teaching the social factors of life which hearing children learn about subconsciously.

Communication, then, is the core of the problem in educating deaf children. Webster defines communication as intercourse by words, letters, or messages, and also as the interchange of thought or opinions.

In considering the communication problem we are talking about, certain distinctions are essential to understand. One is the distinction between language and speech. Language is a particular symbol system that can be expressed in a number of different ways. Speech is one method of utilizing that symbol system, but other methods include writing, printing, and fingerspelling. An individual who knows no Italian might read aloud a paragraph written in Italian well enough for an Italian to understand what he is saying if the proper phonetic markings were indicated, but the individual would still not understand the meaning of the words because he does not understand Italinan. Similarly, teaching a deaf child the speech for a particular word does not in any way guarantee that the child knows the language or the meaning of the word.

The Give and Take of Communication: Not Automatic

Another important distinction to be aware of is the fact that we have expressive communication and receptive communication. We must recognize that they are two different processes and that the skills involved are different for each. A person who has normal hearing and suddenly loses it at age 20 will have no difficulty in terms of his speech or expressive communication. However, because he cannot hear, he may have tremendous difficulty in his receptive communication because he may not be able to speechread very well. On the other hand, although more rarely, a deaf person may not have intelligible speech and yet may be rather highly skilled in lipreading or in the receptive phase of communication. Skill in expression does not automatically ensure skill in reception, nor vice versa.

In any discussion of expressive and receptive communication, most of which is based on language, we should also note that we have internal language as well. This is the ability to handle the symbol system in such a way that cognitive thinking can be carried on.

WHAT IS ORAL AND WHAT IS MANUAL COMMUNICATION?

In educating the deaf, we customarily use certain terminology which is not always completely understood by others not directly concerned. The terminology is confusing because the meaning used in one place is not necessarily the meaning used in some other place.

How Educators Use the Terms

The term oral communication as used by educators of deaf children denotes the teaching of speech as an expressive skill and the teaching of speechreading as a receptive skill. It also means that speech and speechreading are the means of communication used for transmission of thoughts and ideas. The oral educator does not exclude the use of reading and writing, but he does exclude the use of any manual communication. In some but not all oral programs, it is thought that the oral skills should always precede reading and writing.

The term manual communication includes both expressive and receptive forms of communication. It also includes two basic systems: the language of signs, and fingerspelling. In actual practice, frequently both the language of signs and fingerspelling are used in the same communication.

The terms combined or simultaneous means of communication generally mean that, expressively, speech and fingerspelling are used simultaneously, or speech and the language of signs are used simultaneously. On the receptive end, the individual receives the message both through lipreading the speech at the same time as reading the signs or fingerspelling.

How Schools Use the Terms

In addition to this terminology used to identify methods of communication, we also have the words used as a method of classifying schools. A purely oral school completely prohibits the use of manual communication at any time and any place, as far as the children attending the school are concerned. Other schools that are not purely oral may claim they have oral departments. Sometimes all of the educational departments in such a school are oral. This means that as far as the educational program in the classroom is concerned, the school prohibits all manual communication and resorts only to oral means of communication. However, manual communication may be used between children outside the classroom in assembly exercises and other group meetings.

Sometimes, schools with oral departments are referred to as combined schools, but in practice there are a number of different patterns that may be in effect in several different schools, each of which calls itself a combined school. As indicated above, there are certain instances where all of the educational programs are carried on orally but manual communication is allowed outside the classes. Certain other schools establish manual classes for those children generally considered slow learners, while the rest of the classes are oral. Still others conduct all classes of older children as combined classes, with both manual and oral communication, while all classes for the younger children are exclusively oral. Other schools that have a combined or simultaneous system may use the Rochester Method. This means they fingerspell and talk simultaneously regardless of whether communication takes place in the classroom, on the playground, the vocational department, or the assembly hall. The language of signs is not part of the Rochester Method. Some schools may use this system with all the children in the school, and others may use it only with older children, restricting their younger children exclusively to oral means of communication in the classroom.

This multiplicity of specific terminology has caused a great deal of misunderstanding with no agreement in regard to the terms.

Scientific Data Test Some Assumptions

In this long controversy of the past 100 years, there has been no objective data to determine the basis of programs or procedures. As a result there have been certain assumptions made for the basis of the exclusively oral education as practiced by most schools for the deaf in the country, at least as far as their younger children were concerned. There now appears to be a gathering of scientifically obtained data that disprove these assumptions. Following are eight assumptions and the reasons for now considering them invalid:

1. It has been assumed in oral education that expressive and receptive communication was one global entity. Parents or others who continually refer to their desire that a child be taught orally were completely ignoring the fact that oral communication is not one global skill but is composed of at least two very different types of skills in the expressive and receptive phases. We have specific understanding of this today, and we have a great deal of evidence that the two skills may not be present equally in each individual.

2. Demanding that a child's communication be limited to oral means ignores completely the laws of individual differences. We know that children are as different in their ability to learn to talk and to learn to speechread as they are in their ability to learn anything else.

3. The distinction between using speechreading as a receptive means of communication when a person had a command of language as opposed to using speechreading to learn a new language was frequently not recognized. Thus, the effectiveness of speechreading for the postlingually deaf person is much greater than for the prelingually deaf person. The objectives are different. Even the postlingually deaf person has difficulty in understanding because less than 50 percent of the sounds are visible on the lips. However, he has a language background to fill in the gaps. However, the prelingually deaf person has to try to use this highly inefficient input system to try to learn the language. At times when a large percentage of the enrollment of a school for the deaf was postlingually deaf or hard of hearing, speechreading was frequently a good input system for many. Now that most of the enrollment is prelingually deaf, this is a very ineffective input system when used alone for children who have to learn language.

4. It was assumed that manual communication, particularly the language of signs, created the confusion in language that deaf children have. When deaf children use mixed-up language, this is commonly referred to as "deafy" language. The assumption that deafy language results primarily from knowledge of the language of signs has been disproved. Deaf children who never knew the language of signs also make "deafy" mistakes. An analysis of the small number of clues received in speechreading indicates that a person does not see English on the lips. He sees only a few clues and then has to fill in the rest. Thus, speechreading does not result in continued input of straight English, and does not help the child to learn unless there is supplementary input.

5. It has long been assumed that the use of manual communication by a deaf child would make that child less proficient in his own speech and in the use of speechreading. Recent research studies carried on by different investigators in separate parts of the country have disproven this assumption. It has been shown through the studies made by Meadow and by Quigley, among others, that the speech of deaf children who have manual backgrounds is no less intelligible or their understanding of speechreading no less proficient than those of deaf people who had no manual communication.

6. It has been assumed that if a person had the opportunity to use manual communication he would not attempt to use oral communication. Experience has shown that this assumption is not valid. We have been utilizing manual communication and oral communication simultaneously for years, and we find that our students continue to talk and continue to want others who are proficient in manual communication to talk simultaneously with manual communication. This means that our students are benefiting by speechreading added to the manual signs or fingerspelling.

7. It was apparently assumed that if there were any psychological and emotional problems as a result of limited oral communication between the child and his parents, they were not as important as trying to be sure that exclusively oral communication was continued. Both experience and research studies show that major psychological and emotional problems result from lack of communication between parents and child. In addition, there is some evidence that some children develop further emotional problems when the parents reject manual communication. Because this is a communication method the child uses with other children, the child subconsciously feels rejected when the parent punishes him for using manual communication.

8. It has been assumed that pure oralism could not exist where any manualism was allowed. This statement has been made by DiCarlo. So, while a compromise has generally been reached in other areas, in this controversy such a middle ground has not been reached because of the assumption that no compromise is possible without losing the entire battle. If the objective is good oral communication skills, then this assumption is not valid, because those skills are attained by many who utilize a combined, simultaneous method.

These eight assumptions stated above were the basis for three objectives of the exclusively oral educational program:
* that the major communication method used by deaf people would be primarily oral
* that the result of this educational program would be functional as far as the communication skills of most of the deaf children were concerned
* that all deaf people would be primarily a part of the hearing world

Deaf People Communicate Pragmatically If They Can

In actuality we find that deaf people adjust their communication methods according to their own skills and according to the situation in which they find themselves. A deaf person with good expressive communication skills uses them when he is with hearing people. If he does not trust his receptive skills, or has very poor receptive skills, he has hearing people write to him. It is not an all-or-none or an either-or situation as far as a deaf person is concerned. He finds that he has to continue to make adjustments.

Unfortunately, the overall oral communication skills of a great number of deaf adults have not proven to be functional in spite of the fact that nearly all had an oral education during their early school years.

And, finally, deaf people do not live exclusively in a hearing world, nor do they live exclusively in a deaf world. Deaf people generally marry other deaf people. A certain number of them have deaf children, and a larger number have hearing children. Some have other deaf relatives, but a larger number have hearing relatives. Their neighbors are hearing people, and generally they work with hearing people. Most deaf people probably socialize more with other deaf people, and most deaf people find that if they are going to be involved in organized religion, this has to be with a group where other deaf people are involved, and where means of communication are such that they can understand—generally, via manual communication.

Public residential schools for deaf children that pride themselves on being combined schools but actually maintain exclusively oral education for their younger children have been nearly as guilty in producing uneducated deaf people as purely oral schools have been.

That a child could learn expressive and receptive communication orally equally well—that individual differences in young children could be ignored—that a new language could be taught through speechreading as the receptive channel of communication—that oral skills could not develop if manual communication were allowed in primary classrooms—and that emotional problems that arise out of frustrated communication could be disregarded—all these are assumptions that have contributed to the low educational level of deaf people, about which we have all become concerned. These assumptions were generally practiced by combined as well as by oral schools.

TOTAL COMMUNICATION:
ADAPTING THE METHOD TO THE CHILD

Comparing Child Achievement Levels

The evidence seems quite clear that Total Communication is

what is needed for all deaf people from the youngest years to the oldest. Communication is not speech or speechreading alone. Also, it is not vocabulary building or word recognition alone. Communication is the person's ability to use his language for expressing ideas, needs, and feelings. As Meadow points out, a 4-year-old hearing child not only has the vocabulary of 2- to 3,000 words, but in addition, he follows the rules of grammar and syntax that enable him to combine these words in many meaningful ways. The typical deaf child of the same age with exclusively oral communication has only a few words at his command and rarely expands them into expressions for additional meanings.

We generally agree that the early years are tremendously important for all kinds of language and communication learning. This leads to the conclusion that all means should be used to get concepts, ideas, words, and expressions into a child's mind, so that he will have the tools for communication with others and, also, the basic tool necessary for cognitive thinking. Studies of deaf children of deaf parents who had manual communication from their earliest years show these children attain higher levels in school and have better language, and their performance IQ averages are higher. Such children had a head start with communication from their earliest years.

Experimental Classroom Techniques

At our school, younger children carry on finger painting, which is not unusual for any group of young children. If an adult tries to interpret what a child means when he draws a picture, he has little chance, but if the adult can ask the child what he has drawn the child can generally tell him a great deal about it. By allowing our younger children to use any means of communication, including formal signs and in some instances fingerspelling, the teacher could generally find out what the child had in his own mind when making a particular painting. Using this as the basis, the teacher could then write a story based on his picture in English in manuscript form for that individual child. We believe that this is one of the best means of starting to teach beginning reading. It is only through Total Communication that this could be carried on.

At the California School for the Deaf in Riverside, we have had two preschool classes of deaf children between the ages of 3 and 5. We have been teaching them the language of signs and fingerspelling as well as speech, speechreading, and word recognition from the manuscript

> //We find some 3-year-olds using Total Communication have developed 300 usable concepts manually; the typical number for a child using exclusively oral means is likely to be about 20.//

form. We find some 3-year olds have developed as many as 300 usable concepts manually, while the typical number for a child using exclusively oral means is likely to be about 20 in the same period of time. The mothers come to school one day a week and use Total Communication with the children at home. The mothers are highly enthusiastic, because they and their children are really communicating.

We have had many 5-year-old children of deaf parents who come to school with a good background in manual communication. When the child is old enough for the manual fingerspelling to be meaningful, he uses fingerspelling instead of signs when the teacher insists.

Emotional Benefits

Emotional problems may result when a child's mother disappears for several hours and the child has no idea of where she has gone or when she will return. Physically, the child may be quite safe with his older brother or with a babysitter. If the mother can use any means of communication with her child to get across the idea of where she will be and perhaps some idea of when she will return, there is strong likelihood that fewer emotional fears will develop.

One of the most important sequences in every child's learning development is the period of time when he asks the question "why?" Sometimes he really wants to know and other times he doesn't really care, but merely wants an answer that ensures contact. Without Total Communication, deaf children never have an opportunity to go through this learning phase. What effect has such a lack had on the development of the deaf child's cognitive powers?

Educational Benefits

Many articles about education and about teaching frequently emphasize the fact that the good teacher draws out from his pupil information that he already knows, or by skillful questioning and discussion helps the individual to see new relationships he was not aware of before. All of this is predicated on the assumption that a great deal of ability to

> //Without hearing and without knowledge of language, the deaf child has not been able to acquire the information and skills. The important thing is to get information into the child's brain so that he will have it to use.//

use a symbol system is in that student's mind, so the teacher can utilize it. These assumptions are not valid in the case of deaf children. Without hearing and without knowledge of language, the deaf child has not been able to acquire the information and skills for the teacher to draw out. The important thing is to get information into the child's brain so that he will have it to use. It seems logical, then, to use every channel and every vehicle possible to get information and language into the child, so that the teacher will have the opportunity to draw it out again in different forms and, in the educative process, teach the child to think. This means saturation with Total Communication.

REFERENCES

Brill RG: A study in adjustment of three groups of deaf children. Except Child 26: 464-466, 1960

Brill RG: Hearing aspects of deafness. Volta Rev 63: 168-175, 1961

Brill RG: The superior IQs of deaf children of deaf parents. Calif Palms 15: 1-4, 1969

DiCarlo LM: The Deaf. Englewood Cliffs, NJ, Prentice-Hall, 1964

Meadow KP: Early manual communication in relation to the deaf child's intellectual, social and communicative functioning. Am An Deaf 113: 29-41, 1968

Moores DF: Psycholinguistics and deafness. Am An Deaf 115: 37-48, 1970

Morkovin B: Experiment in teaching deaf preschool children in the Soviet Union. Volta Rev 62: 260-268, 1960

Quigley SP: The influence of fingerspelling on the development of language, communication, and educational achievement in deaf children. Institute for Research on Exceptional Children, University of Illinois, 1969

Vernon M; Mental health, deafness, and communication. Md Bull 90: 81-82, 94, 1970

Dr. Brill formally tests some assumptions about deaf children of deaf parents.

The Superior IQ's of Deaf Children of Deaf Parents*

RICHARD G. BRILL

The basic handicap of deaf children, particularly prelingually deaf children, is language. His lack of hearing prevents his acquiring an understanding of language in the way a hearing child does.

For this reason, it is necessary to use nonlanguage intelligence tests, usually performance tests, to obtain a valid measure of a deaf child's intelligence.

In a previous study by this investigator (Brill, 1960), it was found that the mean IQ of a group of 45 children of deaf parents enrolled at the California School for the Deaf, Riverside, was 111.7.

It has frequently been stated by teachers of deaf children that deaf children of deaf parents have a higher rate

*Reprinted from The California Palms (The Publication of the California School for the Deaf, Riverside). 15: 1-4, December, 1969, with permission.

of academic achievement than deaf children of hearing
parents. Until recently, there have been no formal
investigations of this contention. The hypothesis of the
author's study was that deaf children of deaf parents would
have a mean IQ on performance tests of intelligence that was
significantly higher than a representative sample of deaf
children who did not have deaf parents.

REVIEWING THE LITERATURE

In the study reported above, a group of 45 deaf children
of deaf parents, constituting the total number of such
children in the school at the time, was matched with two
other groups. One group was composed of deaf children
who also had deaf siblings, and the other group was composed
of deaf children each of whom was the only deaf child in the
family. In both of the latter groups the parents were hearing.
The groups were matched on an individual basis, taking into
account sex, chronological age, and intelligence quotients.
The average IQ for the base group of deaf children of deaf
parents was 111.7. The members of the other two groups
were then selected on a matching basis.

Another study (Brill, 1962) found that the Wechsler
Intelligence Scale for Children discriminates well in terms of
ultimate academic achievement of deaf students.

Stuckless and Birch (1966) made a study of the
influence of early manual communication on the linguistic
development of deaf children. They selected two groups of
children, one with deaf parents and one with hearing parents.
They selected children from six schools for deaf children and
found a total of 146 deaf children over 7 years old with deaf
parents. In their study, they matched deaf children of deaf
parents with deaf children of hearing parents. The matching
took into account a number of different factors, including
intelligence. By the time they were finished with their
matching, they had reduced the number of deaf children with

deaf parents from 146 to 38. The 38 deaf children of deaf parents had a mean IQ of 102, while the control group, composed of 38 deaf children of hearing parents, had a mean IQ of 104. This does not mean that the average IQ of 102 was the mean of the entire group of 146 deaf children of deaf parents. These 38 had been selected for matching purposes. Stuckless and Birch concluded, "the very young deaf child who is provided a manual communication system develops subsequent reading, written language, and speechreading skills superior to the deaf child without early manual communication."

A recent study by Meadow (1967) was concerned with the effect of early manual communication and family climate on the deaf child's development. In this study a group of 59 deaf children with deaf parents was selected and matched with other children drawn from a pool of approximately 225 deaf children. The mean IQ of the deaf children with deaf parents was 111.5, while the matched group with hearing parents had a mean IQ of 108.9. The 59 deaf children of deaf parents constituted nearly all of the children in this category enrolled at the California School for the Deaf, Berkeley. Thus it is highly representative of that particular group of children. However, the average IQ of the control group was not necessarily representative of the total pool from which those children were drawn.

The Meadow study said "when pairs of children were compared in terms of their scores on the Stanford Achievement Test, the children with deaf parents were found to have an average advantage of 1.25 years of achievement in arithmetic, 2.1 years in reading, and 1.28 years in overall grade achievement. These differences were significant beyond the one percent level of confidence." Results also showed that the gap increased, so that at the senior high-school level, the deaf children of deaf parents had an average advantage of 2.2 years.

TESTING PROCEDURES
AT CALIFORNIA SCHOOL FOR THE DEAF

In the California School for the Deaf, Riverside, during the 1967—68 school year, there were 65 children of a total enrollment of 556 whose parents were deaf.

Of the remainder, the 36 children who were classified as hard of hearing and the 80 children who were classified as having a handicap such as mental retardation or cerebral palsy in addition to deafness were eliminated. From the balance, all of whom were prelingually deaf with hearing parents and no additional handicap, every fourth child was selected from the alphabetical listing of this group. This constituted a representative sample of 98 children.

The parents of all children selected for the study were given a card with the following statements and asked to check one or more of them:
*We used the formal language of signs with our child before he entered school.
*We used manual fingerspelling with our child before he entered school.
*We used both signs and fingerspelling with our child before he entered school.
*We never used signs or fingerspelling with our child before he entered school.

Of the deaf parents of 65 deaf children, only one parent checked the last statement. Thus there were 64 children of deaf parents who had used some form of manual communication with their parents before entering school.

With the 98 deaf children of hearing parents, there were 88 responses from parents indicating they had never used signs or fingerspelling with their child before entering school. These 88 children constituted the comparative sample.

The most recent intelligence test score was selected for a child in this study. These intelligence test scores were either Wechsler Adult Intelligence Scale (WAIS), the Wechsler Intelligence Scale for Children (WISC), or the Leiter Intelligence Scale. Because the Leiter Scale has a mean of 95 instead of 100, a conversion table was used to utilize the Leiter scores on the same scale as the Wechsler scores.

TABLE I
CENSUS OF DEAF CHILDREN
ACCORDING TO IQ TEST RESULTS

Test	Deaf Parents	Hearing Parents
WAIS	5	10
WISC	26	46
Leiter	33	32
	64	88

The Superior IQ's of Deaf Children of Deaf Parents

Generally, the WAIS tests were administered to children between the ages of 16 and 19, the WISC to children between the ages of 9 or 10 and 16, with the Leiter tests administered to children between the ages of 6 and 9. There was an occasional exception to this.

TABLE II RESULTS OF IQ TESTING

Profile	Children with Deaf Parents	Children with Hearing Parents
Number	64	88
Mean	113	104
Standard Deviation	15.2	12.4
Standard Deviation of the Mean	1.9	1.3
Range	64-150	79-140

TEST RESULTS

The mean IQ score for the children with deaf parents was 113, whereas the representative sample of children with hearing parents had a mean IQ of 104. The difference between the two groups was significant at the one percent level of confidence. By inspection of Table III it can be seen that the superiority is general for nearly every age. The number of cases at any individual age is not great enough to make a statistical analysis, but it can be seen that only at age 13 is a group of 8 children of hearing parents superior to a group of 4 children with deaf parents. One of the 4 children with deaf parents in this group had an IQ of 64.

TABLE III MEAN IQ'S FOR DEAF CHILDREN BY AGE

	Deaf Parents		Hearing Parents	
Age	N	M(IQ)	N	M(IQ)
19	1	119	1	105
18	1	109	3	108
17	1	125	4	105
16	5	107	4	102
15	2	123	3	95
14	3	121	7	108
13	4	96	8	107
12	7	109	9	106
11	2	115	7	99
10	4	119	9	112
9	3	115	3	92
8	6	111	9	104
7	15	110	16	100
6	8	121	4	107
5	2	122	1	90
	64M = 113		88M = 104	

The Superior IQ's of Deaf Children of Deaf Parents

It should be pointed out that in selecting the universe for the sample of deaf children of hearing parents, any child with an additional handicap had been eliminated from this group. This means there were no mentally retarded deaf children in the control group. On the other hand, no child, even though he might have additional handicaps, was eliminated from the group of children with deaf parents. If the mentally retarded child with deaf parents had been eliminated from that group the difference would have been greater.

The superiority of the deaf children of deaf parents, as measured by performance-type intelligence tests, was clear, and the hypothesis of the study was confirmed.

WHAT TEST RESULTS MEAN

The basic difference between these two groups is that the deaf children of deaf parents had the advantage of manual communication from a very early age and long before they entered school. The deaf children of hearing parents rarely had the opportunity for manual communication and very little communication of any kind before they were old enough to enter school.

Vernon (1967) in an analysis of many studies of the intelligence of deaf children, made the following statements in regard to performance-scale IQ tests: "It is necessary instead to perceive these tests as excellent nonlanguage measures of the thought process—remembering, abstracting, reasoning, concept forming, etc., which is what the tests actually are. Once they are conceived as measures of the thinking process, i.e., of cognition, it becomes apparent that they do measure the many facets of thinking more comprehensibly than do the very simple laboratory tests generally used for this purpose." He goes on to say,

"Performance-scale IQ tests are the best available nonverbal measures of the thought process."

Bruner (1966) defines cognitive growth as "how human beings increase their mastery in achieving and using knowledge." He goes on to state, "Cognitive growth, whether divergent or uniform across cultures, is inconceivable without participation in a culture and its linguistic community." He says there are three ways in which somebody "knows" something: "1) through doing it, 2) through a picture or image of it, and 3) through some such symbolic means as language."

Deaf children who learn a manual communication system at a very early age are developing a symbolic system even though the symbolism is not necessarily English.

Furth (1966) states, "All thinking activity which is directly concerned with events not perceptually present employs symbols. Symbols serve to broaden the scope of intelligent adaptation across time and place."

CONCLUSION

A deaf child who has the opportunity to learn and use manual communication from a very early age begins his cognitive growth, which makes it possible for him to utilize the various thinking processes as a result of having a symbol system. The deaf child who is prohibited from developing any kind of symbol system which is adequate to his needs does not have the opportunity for similar cognitive growth. The results of the present study suggest that the deaf child of deaf parents has a head start in his development of the thinking processes which is reflected by his scores on a performance intelligence test in later years.

The studies by Meadow and Stuckless and Birch have shown that early manual communication is beneficial to deaf children rather than harmful. This study confirms another aspect of this general conclusion. This suggests that hearing parents should begin to use manual communication with their deaf children during the preschool years.

REFERENCES

Brill RG: A study in adjustment of three groups of deaf children. Except Child 26: 464-66, 1960

Brill RG: The relationship of Wechsler IQs to academic achievement among deaf students. Except Child 28: 315-321, 1962

Bruner JS, Olver RR, Greenfield PM, et al: Studies in Cognitive Growth. New York, John Wiley & Sons Inc, 1966, pp 1-6

Furth HG: Thinking without Language, Psychological Implications of Deafness. New York, The Free Press, 1966, p 224

Meadow KP: The Effect of Early Manual Communication and Family Climate on the Deaf Child's Development. Unpublished doctoral dissertation, University of California, Berkeley, 1967

Stuckless ER, Birch JW: The influence of early manual communication on the linguistic development of deaf children. Am An Deaf 111: 452-60, 499-503, 1966

Vernon M: Relationship of language to the thinking process. Arch Gen Psychiatry 16: 321-333, 1967

Why John's world is so dull and Carol's is so exciting.

Two Children: A Study in Contrasts
•
LAWRENCE NEWMAN

John, an 11-year-old deaf boy, was following his father on a golf course. When he saw me, he excitedly said, "Me watch new!" I asked him what time it was. Pointing to his wrist, he repeated, "Me watch new!" Thinking perhaps I did not make myself clear, I asked him again, in the pictorial uniqueness of sign language "What time is it?" He gave me a vacant, mechanical smile.

This is the same vacant, mechanical smile that deaf people hide behind when they do not understand what is being said to them.

In subsequent conversations with John, I was impressed with the fact that he was a bright boy. Why, then, with his new wristwatch, could he not tell time?

In John's 11 years of physically growing up hadn't his parents or siblings discussed with him the concept of time? And what about the teachers in his school?

John's case is far from unique. Deaf children often begin school at or near a zero point, mentally and educationally speaking. They do not even know their names or the names of commonplace objects. They often do not know how to express themselves, or to figure out what others are saying to them, with the result that they go through a seemingly endless series of frustrations. Their emotional needs are so often ignored that it is no wonder that many deaf adults are said to be maladjusted, to lack responsibility, dependability, or a sense of proper social behavior.

Deaf children may have gone on shopping trips or to the zoo with their parents or teachers, but they remain largely unaffected by what are supposed to be enriching experiences because they have no effective symbol system, or language, to help them codify, classify, and store in their memories all that has happened.

Achievement Level of Deaf Students

The mediocre educational status of deaf people is shocking when measured against their achievement potentials and normal intelligence. Most deaf teenagers reach only a third-grade reading level. The academic achievement scores of deaf students who leave school are on a fifth-grade level, while those of deaf 18- to 20-year old graduates are at approximately an eighth-grade level. Of common knowledge are the seemingly insolvable language problems of deaf children.

WHY EDUCATION BECAME INADEQUATE

From all this, one overriding fact emerges: deafness is more of an educational than a physical handicap. Since the preschool years are the critical learning years, we will be in a better position to take constructive action if we become thoroughly acquainted with background information, and with what goes on during such a period.

Too Much Emphasis on Talk, Talk, Talk

The John Tracy Clinic helped fill the void in the deaf child's preschool years. With its correspondence courses and worldwide fame, it has reached tens of thousands of parents of deaf children and helped many of them. The Tracy Clinic and others like it for preschoolers have followed strictly the oral only philosophy. They have in common what can be called the "Restoration to Society Syndrome."

It is natural for persons with ailments to run to the medical profession for prescriptions, prosthetic devices, and other aids that will make them well again. In the same sense, parents have looked to preschool clinics and programs as refuge centers that will somehow make their children less mute and less deaf. Since the outward manifestations of deafness are the inability to talk and understand the speech of others, the reasoning went that if the deaf child could develop speech and speechreading skills, his deafness would become less noticeable or would not show at all.

Consequently, the prescriptions for preschoolers have been to talk, talk, talk, talk, and to practice speechreading at every opportunity. Hearing aids (the prosthetic devices), speech and speechreading charts, electronic gadgets, tongue depressors, teacher-made aids, and all other aids were brought to bear on the driving goal to help deaf children talk and speechread. All these came under the nomenclature of oral methods. A stigma was attached to the use of sign language, and it was equated with mutism, mental retardation, etc.

Many clinics and programs claimed success in helping the deaf population to talk and speechread. Masked behind this claim of success, however, was the fact that many deaf children already had the ability to speak because they had not been born deaf. They are the postlingually deaf population, those who became deaf after a language base had been formed. The later in life the onset of deafness occurs, the better will be the deaf child's speech.

Not one clinic or program for deaf children experimented with the use of an additional communication tool, manual communication, in order to see if it would help facilitate the development of speech and speechreading and, more importantly, cognitive skills.

Many adult deaf leaders have long known that there was something wrong with the educational system. They constantly met with adult deaf people in their clubs and churches, and in other social and sports activities, and they could see that there was something lacking in their ability to read and write, in their knowledge of world affairs, in their social awareness. Deaf teachers of older deaf children, especially, could see that there was something seriously wrong with the educational development of older deaf students, even though many of these students were postlingually deaf.

Deaf adults were not in positions of authority or influence, nor were they organized enough to cry out or take action against the inadequacies of the educational systems all over the country. Since parents primarily desired their deaf offspring to speak and speechread, they looked askance at manual communication. They felt it was a threat to the acquisition of speech and speechreading skills. Because the majority of deaf adults utilized manual

> //Parents often felt that their children would grow up to be like normal hearing children; therefore, they did not want their deaf children to identify with deaf adults.//

communication, most parents did not want to listen to or cooperate with them. In too many cases, parents felt that their children would grow up to be like normal hearing children; therefore, they did not want their deaf children to identify with deaf adults.

Thus, for a long period of time, deaf leaders, deaf teachers, and many other informed deaf adults stood almost alone in their battle for better education for their deaf children. There were no demands for accountability.

EDUCATIONAL STATUS QUO FACES TWO CHALLENGES

Then, two major trends slowly but inexorably emerged in the field of education of deaf children. One was the growing realization that the deaf population was changing from the postlingually deaf child to the prelingually deaf child; that is, from those who already had a language base to those who were born deaf and had to be taught speech and language both, from scratch. The difficulties and the failures became apparent. School people could no longer hide behind the fact that the reason deaf children could speak was not because of their teaching skills, but because the deaf children already had speech skills, since their hearing had been intact for a crucial period of time.

The second trend was research. In the past, arguments or theories were based on rhetoric, on emotion, on fragmentary evidence. Now, some researchers, namely, Drs. McCay Vernon, Hilde Schlesinger, Kay Meadow, Donald Moores, Richard Brill and Stephen Quigley, undertook various research projects. One recurrent theme emerged: deaf children of deaf parents were academically ahead of deaf children of hearing parents. Also, their speech skills were equivalent, while their speechreading skills were significantly ahead.

Breakthroughs

This was a bombshell to the education of deaf children.

Since almost all deaf parents of deaf children utilized manual communication, it destroyed many myths related to this communication modality. For the first time, preschool clinics and programs, as well as other educational programs for deaf children, found themselves on the defensive. Instead of the oral method, they came up with a new term, aural-oral. The argument they presented was that it is not by speechreading alone, but in conjunction with auditory aids that the deaf child will be able to communicate with a world of the hearing. Their gambit now was to proclaim that better auditory equipment and more intensive auditory training were the deaf child's salvation.

Manual Communication Acquires Status

In the meantime, many events were taking place that helped lessen the stigmata attached to the use of manual communication. The television star, Nanette Fabray, herself nearly deaf without hearing aids, helped glamourize the language of signs and place it on a pedestal it had never before enjoyed. The National Theater of the Deaf and its talented actors and actresses brought manual communication to new heights of ingenuity, beauty, and artistic grace, while, at the same time, demonstrating its potential and flexibility before thousands of people all over the world.

In an atmosphere of enlightenment and acceptance, people began to experiment with new and expanded forms of manual communication. New signs were invented for words where none existed before, and there came into existence signs for tenses and verb endings. Following in the original footsteps of David Anthony, a deaf man, efforts were made all over this country to bring the language of signs to a closer representation of English.

Educators Take a Fresh Look

Professionals in the field of education began to take a searching look into what they were doing. Doubts were cast on many methods usually taken for granted. Probing questions were asked. Self-evaluations and reevaluations were undertaken. Roy Holcomb, a deaf man, was put in charge of a school program in Santa Ana, California. He helped initiate and spread the concept of Total Communication. David M. Denton, superintendent of the Maryland School for the Deaf, made a forthright stand and proclaimed his school's total commitment to Total Communication.

Most importantly, hearing parents of preschool deaf children became more informed and knowledgeable. They began to learn manual communication and to utilize the concept of Total Communication with their one-to five-year old children. They met instant success, and in a short while, a new nationwide parent organization, the Convention of American Instructors of the Deaf Parent Section, came into being. This group is also known as the International Association of Parents of the Deaf.

Progress to Date

Although many changes for the better continue to take place, one must keep in perspective the reality of the present state of affairs. Most teacher-training centers still do not make it mandatory for trainees to have at least some rudimentary skill in manual communication. The majority of parents of deaf children continue to be misled and ill informed, and there is little real communication going on in the families of these children. Teachers in most schools and programs for deaf children, especially teachers of younger children, still do not know how to communicate effectively with those they are supposed to teach. Too many administrators and educators still lack an understanding of manual communication's place in education. They have little or no sensitivity to its worthiness and effectiveness.

Instead of appreciating the fact that the great majority of deaf consumers have and continue to utilize manual communication, which should indicate that it has something powerful going for it, many professionals continue to circumnavigate the issue by coming up with something such as cued speech, the initial teaching alphabet, different facets of aural-oral methods; in short, anything but manual communication itself.

//John never really had any effective family or teacher communication, nor did he have an effective symbol system that could help him understand the world around him.//

With such a background, perhaps we can now better understand why John, a bright boy, could not tell what time it was. John never really had any effective family or teacher communication, nor did he have an effective symbol system that could help him understand the world around him.

Can we really teach the deaf preschool child? Are hearing preschoolers really learning from teachers, or from family members and such media as television, radio, records, and the daily conversations swirling around them? Do all children learn by guidance and osmosis through life experiences rather than by the superimposition of learning tasks by adults?

CAROL'S STORY

Diary of Progress

I have a deaf preschool child, Carol Lee. She was four years old on March 14, 1973. On an almost daily basis I have kept records of her expressions and made notes of her mental, emotional, and social progress since she was eight months old. In addition, on alternate months for a number of years we went to the Salk Institute at La Jolla, California, where world-renowned linguists, Drs. Ursula Bellugi and Edward Klima, made videotape records of Carol Lee's language development. During the other months, these two linguists came to our home with their equipment. Thus, the language development of our deaf preschooler was documented on a monthly basis for over two years.

Carol Lee is only one deaf preschooler, but it is possible to study one individual to the n t h degree and come up with basic conclusions that have universal applications while, of course, taking into account the variables involved.

Since we had four hearing children, we did not expect a deaf child, nor did we discover our daughter was deaf until she was eight months old. Our immediate concern was to establish an effective line of communication with her, to reach and stir a mind that was a veritable tabula rasa. What were we to do with a deaf child without language, without the means to receive and convey thoughts in the normal way? How could our deaf child be helped to learn language and thus become attuned and responsive to the world of the hearing?

Our primary concern was not to help our child talk and speechread, but to catalyze thought and language. Thought produces language; it fills the child with a need to express himself, and the freer he is to do so, the greater the chance for success.

Since moving plastic birds and butterflies attract an infant's eyes, we placed such mobile units over our daughter's playpen. Next came learning toys based on graduations of size and matching of different shapes. She learned to sort things, to count, and to do simple puzzles.

In fact, it turned out that Carol would rather play with jigsaw puzzles than with dolls.

We had some difficulty at first, but, finally, we were permitted to enroll her in a branch of the International Montessori Schools, where a large part of learning was based on nonverbal tasks. Here was a school that emphasized sorting, categorizing, and classifying, that allowed a child to make choices and to move at his own pace. That so few schools and programs have tried to emulate the Montessori methods is a cause for concern and puzzlement.

> //It seems logical that a child's mind be stimulated by nonverbal tasks as early as possible, so that skills develop to perceive patterns, relationships, and associations.//

It seems logical that a child's mind be stimulated by nonverbal tasks as early as possible, so that there will be recognition and perception, the development of skills to perceive patterns, relationships and associations.

This kind of development creates the conditions for thinking, and for an awareness of what people are saying and doing. It lays the groundwork for speechreading skills and for practically all forms of learning.

At the outset, we felt that Carol should have a symbol system that was visually oriented and almost tangible so that she would have a means of expressing herself, of understanding what her parents were talking about with a minimum of ambiguity, and for storing in her memory identifications of familiar objects, persons, and incidents that occurred. It is almost impossible for a prelingually deaf child of two years to speak or speechread squirrel or crocodile, but it is possible to sign them or recognize the signs for them at an age earlier than two.

When we changed Carol's diapers we made the signs for <u>Mommy</u>, <u>Daddy</u>, <u>love</u>, and <u>you wet</u>?, the type of native sign language now called Ameslan, an acronym for American Sign Language, used by deaf people for generations. Here was gross movement and three-dimensional appearance in space that a deaf infant's eyes will follow, will learn to distinguish, and to associate with something relevant. It would appear that no other communication method in the world can equal hand signs in richness, ingenuity, grace, and flexibility. Daily, we brought to our child a live "Sesame Street."

A baby has immediate needs to be cuddled and fed, and, if it can hear, to be spoken to. If the baby cannot hear, common sense dictates that we do more than just mouth words, more than just hope that a hearing aid will take care of everything. This is not to say that a child will not benefit from auditory training, but such training takes time. In the meantime, an effective means of communication must go on in the here and now. Moreover, there is no assurance which child will benefit from auditory training to the extent that it will be as functional as hearing itself. Too many variables are involved, and it could happen that two children may have nearly the same hearing loss delineated on an audiogram, yet one child will hear better than the other.

Holding our Carol near a campfire, we both vocalized and signed the word <u>hot</u>. There was no response, but two weeks later, back home from a vacation trip, she put her hand on our clothes dryer and made the sign for <u>hot</u>.

Input is the first stage. Parents and educators often expect immediate output or performance, and if this is not forthcoming they feel they have not reached the child, or have failed, which, of course, is not true. After two

> //Carol Lee, at ten months, could sign for Daddy, but this was the same sign for Mommy. It took two more months before she could make a different sign for each.//

months of input, our daughter, at ten months, made the sign for Daddy, but this was the same sign for Mommy. It took two more months of input before she could make a different sign for each.

Between 16 and 22 months, Carol's single word sign production grew rapidly to 60 words. Of course, she quickly learned the signs for candy, cookie, ice cream. She also had signs for dog, cat, wrong, pretty, more, dirty, and for two-word combinations, such as "Daddy work," "cookie eat," "me funny," "boy laughing." She could tell us which drink she wanted: water, milk, soda pop, or orange juice. When I asked hearing parents of deaf children how they knew which drink their child wanted, I was told, "By pointing."

Carol's Language Statements

What is intriguing is the way Carol uses the same sign in a spiral form as she grows older and becomes more aware of subtle shades of meanings. "More Cookie" becomes "Pull up socks more." She uses the same sign in a different context. For example, with the sign for finish, she will say "finish sat," "finish bathroom," or "finish sleep." It has been fascinating to watch her expressions expand from single to two, three, and now several word-sentence statements, such as, "Me swim, sleep, wake up, eat cookie cookie." With mouth imitating the whir of an airplane, she said, "Father fly finish, come Sunday." As the months passed, she became more receptive to correct grammatical forms, with her family members serving as models. With constant

FIGURE 1 Lawrence Newman bringing daughter Carol "a live Sesame Street."

input and modeling she made correct language statements, such as "I am sorry," "I want some cake," and "Do you love me?"

Bellugi and Klima made videotape records and studied the language development of deaf children of deaf parents at the Salk Institute in La Jolla, California. In their article, "The Roots of Language in the Sign Talk of the Deaf," Psychology Today, June, 1972, they write that one of the Children, Pola, has in her early combination of signs the "full range of semantic relations expressed by hearing children." They also found "a steady increase in the length of her signed sequences that matches the increase found in hearing children," and that it seemed "in spite of the change in modality, the milestones of language development may be the same." They noted that "The vocabulary of sign language makes many more discriminations about ways of looking and seeing than spoken English does."

To have a sense of perspective, we need to compare the progress of a deaf child with that of a hearing child. A hearing child at the age of 18 months has a 25-word vocabulary, while a deaf child customarily has no vocabulary or understanding. A hearing child at the age of two or three understands directions, uses short sentences, asks questions, relates experiences, understands adults well, and has a 500-word vocabulary, while a deaf child has a vocabulary of a few words, and yells or screeches to express desires or wants (Little, 1970).

Carol identifies each sibling in our family by the first letter of his or her name. For example, she forms the letter "R" with her fingers and shakes it to stand for her sister, Rochelle. Bojo, our dog, was abbreviated to "BJ." She became curious and began to fingerspell such words as: off, OK, no jump, hole, and oh. At one time she broke a drinking glass. I scolded her and told her to be careful. She fingerspelled back "OK." She would fingerspell words from books, newspapers, or even from the walls of toilets. Surely, the foundation for reading readiness was being laid.

Deaf students have difficulty understanding the abstract. We taught Carol the sign for flower and added the sign for beautiful. When she received a new blue coat with a furry collar, she exclaimed in sign "Beautiful!" Her ability to use on her own power an abstract notion in a different context is, I think, unusual for a deaf child of her age.

Carol's Emotional Development

Because we established an effective line of communication with our daughter, we think we have laid the groundwork for good physical, emotional, and mental health. We can reason with her: "Eat first, candy later." How many times, in frustration, have parents and others in the field of the education of deaf children slapped unnecessarily or without explanation?

When Carol was ill she was able to use the sign for <u>hurt</u> near her ear or her stomach to tell us exactly what was bothering her. At one time, as I was leaving her room, she made the sign for <u>leave</u>. Frozen in my tracks, I tried to figure out what she meant. It soon dawned on me that she wanted me to leave the lights on. She was not even two years old, yet she could tell us that she was not reluctant to go to sleep, but just did not want to be left alone in the dark.

How does a parent make sure a deaf child understands that something is dangerous and can cause injury? We discussed with Carol what would happen if one were hit by a car and, therefore, how important it was to look both ways before crossing the street. In no time we caught her walking to the edge of a sidewalk. She stopped and signed to herself "look both ways," then she crossed her arms, rested them on her chest, and looked up and down the street several times before crossing.

At nearly four years of age, Carol had a vocabulary that approached 1,000 words. She can string out sentences orally, manually, or simultaneously, in crude but meaningful ways. But this does not tell the whole story—far from it.

Interactions

As cherry blossoms come to bloom, so Carol's mind begins to flower, the best and most important part. When she was only a little over a year and a half she wanted a book which her brother was sitting on. He would not get up, so she threw a ball to divert his attention and thus grab the book. Because she was given an effective visual and expressive symbol system, she has been able to recall past events—the animals visited at the zoo, the Railroader, a restaurant where we all ate together, the visit to her grandparents. An internal language structure seems to be developing within her rather than being superimposed upon her by drills and imitation. She is able to invent and generate language when there is a pressing need to express something, such as her desire for a milkshake, ketchup, the opposite of the word long. She is able to manipulate her thoughts into expressions that make sense. She gave me a piece of gum and when I greedily asked for another, she said, "You pig, fat you pig." Coming from a hearing child,

> //Coming from a hearing child, Carol's action would have invited a spanking. Coming from a deaf child it seems like a miracle, like a soul set free to communicate joyously.//

this would invite a spanking. Coming from a deaf child it seems like a miracle, like a soul set free to communicate joyously.

Carol understands directions, asks and answers questions, relates experiences, peeps in and understands the conversations of others. She enjoys herself and takes pleasure in herself. (Our next door neighbor said she is the happiest baby he has ever seen.) She is free to use her hands or to use her voice. She will sign to the ocean waves, saying, "stay, stay," as they creep near her mudpies. She will talk to herself or to her dog, urging him to eat. She will yell at her Daddy with her hands, saying, "bad, bad, bad," if he drives away without taking her. She was toilet trained before the age of two. Because there was reciprocal communication, we could tease each other, and when she entered preschool her sense of humor showed.

WE ASK OURSELVES: WHAT DID WE DO RIGHT?

Both my wife and I are teachers, but we kept formal teaching to a minimum, because we are aware of the importance of being parents first, and because Carol herself rebels at any formal teaching on our part. We kept communication spontaneous, natural, and fun. As our daughter moved through different levels of readiness we mixed Ameslan with fingerspelling and added the new signs in current use, such as the signs that distinguish bus, car, truck, and those for verb endings and tenses. There was no need to be extreme in any one system, but to try to meet her communication needs as the months went by.

If we had vocalized alone, could we have succeeded as well? There is no doubt in our minds that we could not have, because moving hands are attention getting for children whose ages are measured in months. We deaf people place extra burdens on our eyes to clue us in on what goes on around us. Our eyes are constantly searching for clues or hints or revealing motions other people make. Lip movements are the smallest in the animated category, the most ambiguous, and the most difficult to follow in the communication process. If this is true for deaf adults, how much more so for babies and young children!

What about auditory training? We think it would be as fatal a mistake to depend on auditory methods <u>alone</u> as it would be to depend on any other method <u>alone</u>. Deaf children are not circus animals to be trained to jump through a hoop. When one has impaired hearing, sound becomes muffled or distorted, and the higher the volume produced by the hearing aid, the less one hears. One begins to feel in terms of vibrations, making it exceedingly difficult to understand connected speech. Of course, one can have a set of sentences amplified on and on until one is able to distinguish them by sound clues. This is fine, as long as it is one part of the communication method, and not <u>the</u> communication method. One should not be misled by pockets of success, because there are many factors involved that are difficult to measure, such as the type and kind of hearing loss, extent of other neurological, psychological, and physical damage. The real test comes not in the classroom, but in the extent of functional usage of hearing in the real world.

As mentioned before, the deaf child must have effective communication now, and not after he is trained. There is no documented evidence or nonbiased evaluation that will support the claims that those deaf children with a profound hearing loss can be trained to hear in a functional manner.

We Believe in Total Communication

With our daughter, we followed the philosophy of Total Communication. This is not the Simultaneous method alone, although it is part of it. We would sign and speak a sentence, speak without signing the same sentence, and then speak and sign the same sentence for the third time. Signs, speech, and speechreading reinforce one another. Carol's mother would sing "Rock-a-Bye-Baby," and Carol would sign in unison: then Carol would try to sing it with her mother signing the nursery rhyme. Or we would all sing and sign at the same time.

We did not force our daughter, but gradually led her to the wearing of a hearing aid, even though she has more than a 90 db loss. Once a week she has an hour session with an audiologist, in addition to the part-time, aural-oral methods utilized in her Total Communication preschool class.

Carol has had two teachers. One, who received her training at the Central Institute for the Deaf, stated that Carol could speechread in one month what it took other deaf children a whole year to learn. She also mentioned that

Carol speaks and forms many words normally. Her other teacher wrote:

> "She will spontaneously vocalize if the words are familiar to her. Our big emphasis is on using speech and signs together. She is a very good speechreader. She can speechread all the words written under reading skills and classroom directions. She does well in using all avenues and also speechreads well in spontaneous conversation."

At home, we encouraged her to talk, and many times we talked to her without signing to give her practice in speechreading. We seldom made any formal attempts to teach her such skills, but allowed them, instead, to develop in a natural way. Because we placed no restriction on communication methods, our daughter was able to absorb and give out a lot more than would ordinarily be the case. There was some kind of snowball effect. We sang "Santa Claus Is Coming to Town," and she would be able to copy us. For a profoundly deaf child not yet four years old, the depth and quality of communication seemed remarkable.

IS SPEECH THE MAIN ISSUE?

This question comes to mind: at what point in time should a deaf child be formally taught speech? Should not an effective line of communication first be established under the umbrella of total communication? Should not pains first be taken to see that there is a stimulating environment so that the gears in a deaf child's mind will mesh and he can become a spontaneously communicating and responsive individual? When proper developmental sequences are followed, will there then be more readiness and receptiveness for the aural-oral method? Have the people in the field of education missed the boat by insisting upon and forcing aural-oral methods alone, at the wrong time, and for too prolonged a duration? Here lies the crux of the matter. More scientific research should be brought to bear on this.

Researchers, Educators, and Parents Reply

Drs. Hilde Schlesinger and Kay Meadow, in their research study Sound and Sign (1973), stated that little attention has been paid to the motoric-speech relationship. What is it, for instance, that causes hearing babies to wave their hands when they say, "bye-bye?" She made a clinical study of four families with deaf children—two pairs of hearing parents and two pairs of deaf parents—and found that when manual communication was used early, the deaf children began to use their speech more and their signs less. Schlesinger stated that if parents accepted the child-preferred mode of communication, the child would use other methods through association pathways. This is the antithesis of what is presented to parents. "If you let your child use his hands he will not learn to talk."

It is interesting to note that in Schlesinger's research on 40 preschool children, she found that more than 50 percent of parents complained about frustration involving understanding, 15 percent could not understand the child, and 38 percent could not be understood by the child. The percentage increased as the child grew older.

Professionals in the field of the education of deaf children tell us that one reason deaf children of deaf parents are ahead of deaf children of hearing parents is that the children are accepted quickly, while hearing parents go through traumatic stages of guilt, despair, and then search for remedies which will somehow minimize their child's hearing loss, or restore him or her to society. How true this is remains to be seen, but it serves to divert parents from the basic cause of what is stunting the educational, emotional, and social progress of their deaf children. Once parents can get at the basic cause, there is no reason why the initial shock cannot be overcome and real progress made. In fact, a growing number of hearing parents are doing as well as deaf parents, if not better.

The basic cause is the lack of effective communication in the home during the first few years of the deaf child's life. The rejection of one of the communication modalities, manual communication, is a contributing factor. As Bellugi and Klima (1972) state:

> Sign language, it is clear, is far more than mystical hand waving. Its range and diversity permit humor and pun, song and poetry, whimsy, and whispering. What it lacks in comparison with spoken English it amply compensates for in other ways. The study of sign language gives us insight into the structure of language and the universality of communication, but even more it attests to the richness of human intelligence and imagination.

I suspect that even after counseling, attendance at preschool clinics, associations with others in similar circumstances, too many parents feel inadequate or unable to cope with their deaf offspring. Basically, this is a result of insufficient information parents receive. They are not made aware of alternatives or options if one method is found to be inadequate.

What is needed are training centers for parents of deaf children that will show how Total Communication can be used effectively in the home. With a shelf full of communication tools at their disposal, parents will be in a better position to select one or change from one to the other, according to the varying needs at their children's differing age levels.

The following comments of John and Fleana Snapp, parents of a five-year-old deaf daughter, are worth mentioning here:

Communication in our family means using the language which comes to us in a comfortable way. All of our ideas, fleeting thoughts, desires, opinions, scoldings, and praises are expressed using Total Communication. We feel that the spontaneity of our communication is the essence of its value to us. Rachel sometimes reminds us of our errors in transmission, or that, somehow, she did not get the message. We then try harder to insure that she is included as a full member of "the inner circle." The off-the-cuff comments that you have heard and used every day for years need to be understood by every member of a family. For example, "Someone is at the door," "Ask Bobby to stop barking," "Daddy will be home in a little while and I forgot to thaw out dinner" are some of the quick utterances that are lost to the deaf child unless you use Total Communication. They add a completeness to the child's life which cannot be gotten elsewhere, and it cannot be faked. Total Communication between parent and child, teacher and child, sister and sister, or brother and sister is absolutely mandatory if our children are to get the subtle nuances from life that give meaning to an otherwise drab, statistical world.

Happily, we share the everyday happenings, in detail, with Rachel. Many families take for granted that their children are receiving these details, when, in fact, they are not even being sent.

The Snapps' daughter has made such statements as "The fire is blazing," "Santa will not be confused," and "I am going to have a fit." This family's immersion in Total Communication since their Rachel was a baby has made possible such language expressions, practically unheard of in a prelingually, profoundly deaf five-year-old.

In the meantime, our own deaf daughter's academic progress at approximately three-and-a-half years of age has been noted by her teacher:

> In reading readiness activities Carol is doing exceptional work. She can read her name, her classmates' and teacher's names, and sight-read the following words: boy, girl, mother, father, house, car, dog, cat, Halloween, pumpkin, jack-o-lantern....She knows her alphabet and is learning many of the sounds. Carol can work puzzles (even a 28-piece new puzzle all on her own). She can recall two missing objects from a group of objects.... Her calendar concept is growing and her awareness of the days of the week.... In math she is showing understanding of empty sets (zero) and of equivalent sets. She shows good understanding of comparative words. Her cognitive ability is outstanding. She has a quick and intensive mind. In language she is showing quick growth in vocabulary....

HOW TO RAISE THE STANDARDS FOR ACHIEVEMENT

Again, because Carol had an effective communication symbol system, her input capacity continually expands. Her development and that of the Snapp child parallel a hearing child's, because unrestricted communication tools were made available to quench a child's thirst to know. It is doubtful that a preschool child can really be taught much in a formal way, but he can be mentally stimulated and guided into learning. Daily family communication is the most effective source.

We should no longer be satisfied if a deaf child

knows a few words or can speak a few words. He has the same, normal intelligence as a hearing child, and we should raise our expectations to the point where we can say that his achievement approximates or is equal to that of hearing children.

We have to stop being misled by success stories of those brought up by one communication method alone. Deafness brings with it so many complex problems of an educational, social, and psychological nature that it is foolish to take chances by using only one method of communication to the exclusion of all others. Because aural-oral methods, as well as fingerspelling and signs, come under the umbrella of Total Communication, this is geared to do the greatest good for the greatest number.

What are we afraid of and what is holding us back from zeroing in on the preschool-age child in order to study his progress? If most of our time and energies, and if most research studies were devoted to this critical age, we would begin seeing the light at the end of the tunnel.

REFERENCES

Bellugi U, Klima ES: The roots of language in the sign talk of the deaf. <u>Psychology Today</u> 6: 61-64, 76, 1972

Little JA, ed: <u>Answers</u>. Santa Fe, NM, New Mexico School for <u>the Deaf</u>, 1970, 20-22

Schlesinger H, Meadow K: Sound and Sign. Berkeley, University of California Press, 1972

Part IV:
SIGN LANGUAGE: ITS VARIATIONS AND ITS RELATIONS TO ENGLISH

The traffic between sign languages and English.

ASL and Siglish: The Various Forms of Sign Language
●
LOUIE J. FANT, Jr.

COMMUNICATION SYSTEMS FOR DEAF PEOPLE DEFINED

The term sign language is generic, and covers a wide range of functions. There are several sign languages used by deaf people in the United States, by deaf people in other countries, by hearing people such as the American Indians, and even the gestures of hearing people, particularly of Latin America and the Near East. As a result there are numerous terms which specify each sign language. To the uninitiated, the many terms used can be quite confusing, so definitions are in order.

ASL

These are the initials for American Sign Language, the typical language deaf people use when conversing among themselves. ASL has a unique grammatical structure. It is more similar to Chinese than English, in that each sign represents an entire concept, not just one word.

Ameslan

Ameslan is an acronym for ASL that is identical to ASL in meaning. It is a newly coined word and not yet widespread. It was coined to lend more dignity to the language than initials can and to provide a convenient device with which to refer to other sign languages of the world—Brislan, Russlan, or Argeslan, for example.

Sign

Sign is another term for ASL, identical in meaning to ASL and Ameslan.

Fingerspelling

Use of the manual-alphabet to spell words is called fingerspelling. The manual alphabet consists of a single hand configuration for each letter of the English alphabet. Thus, any English word may be fingerspelled. The manual alphabets of other languages conform to the written alphabets of those languages.

Manual English

A combination of signs and fingerspelling which adheres closely to English grammatical structure, manual English differs from Ameslan in that Ameslan has its own structure, as a language. Thus manual English is only a manual-visual representation of the English language.

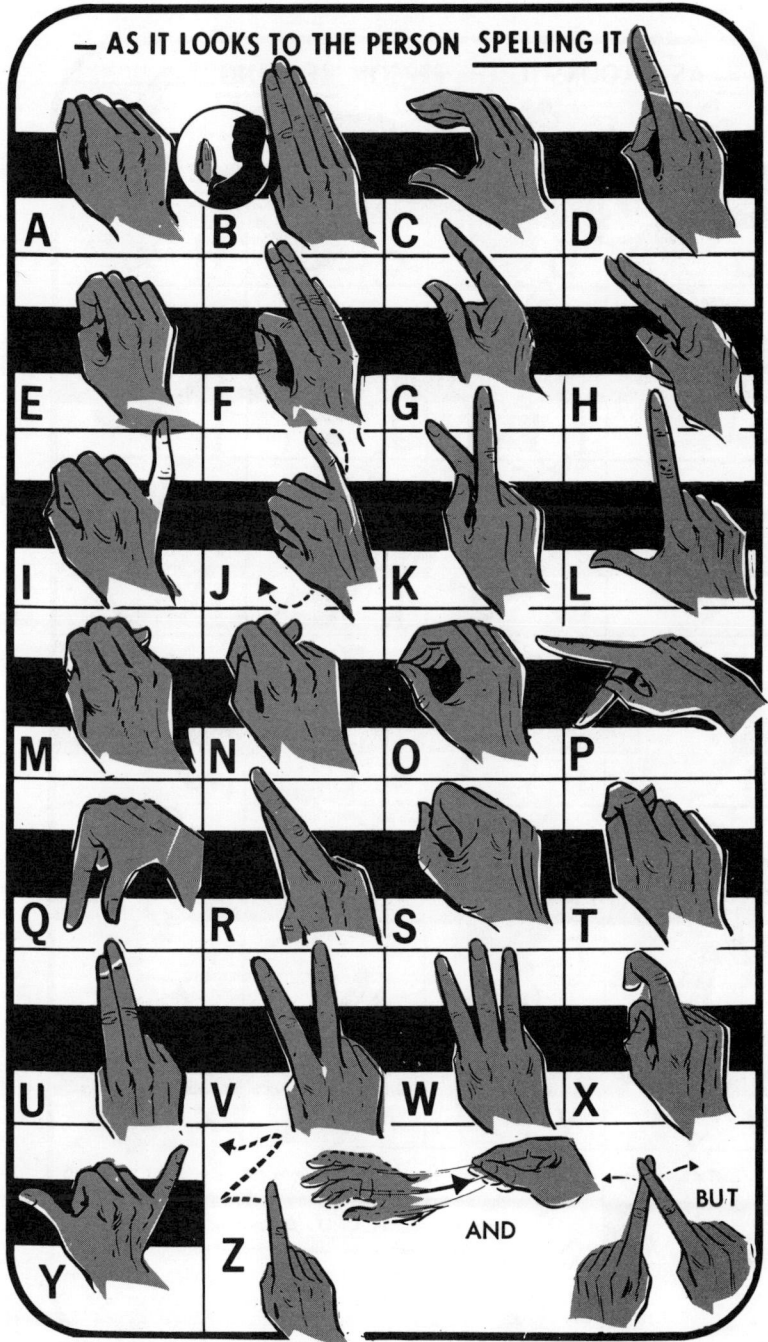

FIGURE 1 The manual alphabet seen by the person spelling it. (Copyright © 1964 by David O. Watson, author of Talk with Your Hands. Reprinted by permission.)

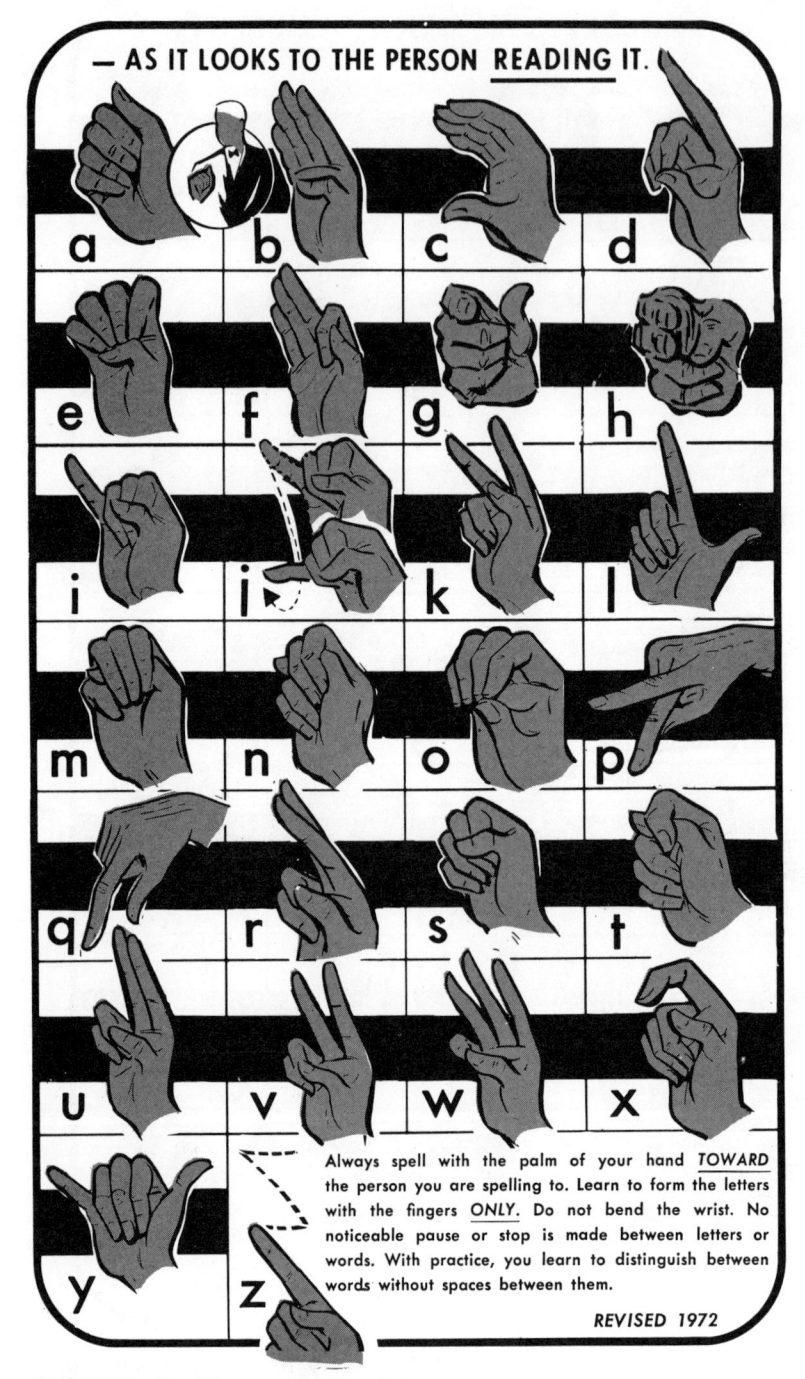

FIGURE 2 The manual alphabet, seen by the person reading it. (Copyright © 1964 by David O. Watson, author of Talk with Your Hands. Reprinted by permission.)

Siglish

Siglish is an acronym for signed English. Actually there are at least two siglishes, defined below under SEE and VE. The difference between the siglishes and manual English is that in the former there is no fingerspelling.

SEE

The initials for two siglishes, Signing Exact English and Seeing Essential English. They are identical and differ in name only. SEE is a siglish, that is, an anglicization of Ameslan. Numerous new signs have been coined to make possible a one-to-one correspondence between signs and words. For example, in Ameslan, there is one sign, eat, which means: eats, eating, eaten, and ate. In SEE, the basic sign, eat, is made, and then a second sign follows to indicate which tense is meant in English.

VE (LOVE)

The initials for Visual English are VE, which is a shortening of L O V E, the Linguistics of Visual English. VE is a siglish and, in concept, is identical to SEE. The difference is that VE breaks down an English word into smaller units, each unit having a corresponding sign.

SOME COMMENTS ON SEE AND VE

*These siglishes were developed in an attempt to teach English to deaf children.

*They are manual-visual representations of English, not languages.

*They differ from manual English in that manual English uses few signs that are not standard Ameslan and uses fingerspelling extensively.

*They avoid fingerspelling on the premise that it is too difficult for preschool deaf children to handle efficiently.

*They are new movements in education of deaf children, centered primarily in California.

*It is too soon to evaluate their efficiency in helping deaf children learn English. Indeed, professional educators are widely divided as to the positive and negative effects they may have on the linguistic development of deaf children.

Rochester Method

This method is communication by fingerspelling and speech only to the exclusion of all signs.

Simultaneous Method

This method communicates by fingerspelling and speech. In general, this approach refers to simultaneous use of manual English and spoken English. SEE, VE, and the Rochester

Method also use spoken English simultaneously.

Combined Method

The Combined Method refers to a philosophy whose proponents follow a purely oral approach to the preschool and primary grades, but permit manual communication in the upper grades. In older literature, it was sometimes used synonymously with the Rochester Method.

Cued Speech

Recently developed cued speech employs a newly devised set of gestures representing all the sounds of English in combination with speech. Actually, it is a technique to facilitate lipreading.

International Sign Language

An attempt to arrive at a set of signs which will be understood by deaf people of all nations, International Sign Language is a project of the World Federation of the Deaf.

> //For most deaf people, Ameslan is their first language, the language in which they feel most comfortable and fluent.//

WHY AMESLAN IS THE FIRST LANGUAGE OF DEAF PEOPLE

For most deaf people, Ameslan is their first language. That is to say, it is the language in which they feel most comfortable and fluent. For most deaf people, English is their second language. Only a small group, perhaps about 10 percent, become completely fluent in English. This is no reflection on their intelligence, ambition, or education, but rather on the tremendous impact that deafness has on English acquisition.

Totally Visual System Is Easier To Learn

Ameslan is far easier for a deaf child to master than English or the siglishes, probably because it is a totally visual language. The siglishes, though they are presented via a visual medium are, nevertheless, representations of English, which is based on sound.

Ameslan: A Rich Language

Ameslan is a full, expressive, and beautiful language. Critics of Ameslan contend that it does not have enough signs to cover all the words in the English language, but they overlook the fact that a sign stands for a concept, not an English word. It is true that there are many concepts for which there are no signs, but these particular concepts do not play an important part in the everyday life of deaf people. Take, for instance, the concept atom. Ameslan has no sign for atom—because most deaf people simply do not need it. The concept arises so infrequently in their lives that they do not bother to invent a sign for it; instead, they fingerspell it. In a college class in physics, however, the concept atom is likely to arise frequently; consequently, a sign for it will probably be coined. In short, Ameslan can be expanded to accomodate whatever conditions a situation presents.

Why Ameslan Remains Unrecognized

Perhaps the major reason Ameslan has not been accorded due recognition as a language is because it has no written form. Dr. William C. Stokoe of Gallaudet College has devised a notation system which makes possible a nearly complete transcription of signs. It falls short of a complete transcription in that the Ameslan's nonverbal components

> //Ameslan's nonverbal components cannot be adequately recorded. The nonverbal elements play a far more crucial role in Ameslan than they do in English.

(facial expression; head, shoulder, and torso movements; speed of the signs, etc.) cannot be adequately recorded. The nonverbal elements play a far more crucial role in Ameslan than they do in English. The only complete way to record Ameslan is through motion-picture films.

It is important that a deaf child learn early in life that a language exists uniquely his own—a language of which he can be proud. Deaf children generally develop very poor images of themselves. One major way to correct this is to show respect for their language. If hearing people give it its proper regard, the deaf child's self esteem will rise. If he is encouraged to excel in it, then he will be more sympathetic toward and eager to acquire English. To deny the deaf child his own language too often fosters a negative attitude toward learning English.

TOTAL COMMUNICATION:
THE BEGINNING OF AN ANSWER

From the beginning, education of deaf children in the United States concerned itself primarily with speaking, reading, and writing English. These areas received the major focus simply because they are the functions most affected by deafness. Yet during the century and a half since its inception, the education of deaf children has made few significant breakthroughs. The state of the art of education is pretty much the same now as it was then. This is not a result of laziness, nor a lack of creative, ambitious educators. It is the same because the dimensions of the problem are enormous and complex. To be sure, there have been tremendous technological advances in hearing aids, and medical science has made important contributions toward preventing and treating deafness. The actual teaching of English (speaking, reading, and writing), however, has progressed very little.

The latest innovation, which promises to achieve better results for English language teaching, is Total Communication. Total Communication is a philosophy of education, not a technique or method of teaching. In its simplest terms, Total Communication means that all modes, or any mode of communication (speech, lipreading, hearing, Ameslan, manual English, the siglishes, fingerspelling, gesture, mime, drawing, pictures, writing, etc.) must be encouraged and exploited to get freeflowing communication started in the deaf child.

The primary goal of the education of deaf children has always been the development of English in the deaf child. The only new emphasis brought to this task by Total Communication is that no mode of communication is to be excluded. The pure oralists, naturally, remain outside the movement. But of those who consider themselves part of it, there are sharp differences on how to use Total Communication to achieve the stated goal of knowing English.

TWO POINTS OF VIEW TOWARD TOTAL COMMUNICATION

Basically, there are two major schools of thought. Their goals are identical, but their philosophies and techniques differ greatly. Yet both schools see themselves as part of the Total Communication movement. One school proposes to develop in the deaf child his own language, Ameslan, and then later to use his language to develop English.

The other school would immerse the deaf child only in English from the beginning. This may be achieved by using fingerspelling exclusively or manual English, or a siglish, or any of these in combination.

It is too soon yet to offer much empirical evidence to prove conclusively which school of thought is right. In the final analysis, it will probably be learned that one approach works for some deaf children, the other is best for others, and either works for some. In that event, a school that purports to use Total Communication would be one where each deaf child would be provided with the approach best for him.

INTERPRETING FOR DEAF PEOPLE

The interpreter plays one of the most important roles of all in bringing together deaf and hearing people. The interpreter is the bridge, the liaison, who facilitates sharing knowlege, information, and experiences between the two groups. Yet it is an unfortunate fact that there are few truly competent interpreters relative to the need. The primary source of competent interpreters has been sons and daughters of deaf parents. This source has never produced an adequate supply of competent interpreters, yet virtually nothing was done to train more until just a few years age. Today, there are numerous educational and vocational training opportunities available for deaf people which were nonexistent ten years ago. There are not, however, enough competent interpreters to maximize the benefits deaf people can gain from these opportunities.

The Registry of Interpreters for the Deaf (RID) is the national professional organization of interpreters. The RID was created partially in response to the need to organize training programs and certification procedures which would increase the flow of competent interpreters. The establishment of the RID was a significant break with the tradition that good interpreters were born, not made.

The Rationale For Precise Terms

It is necessary to digress again to define a few more terms. The RID defines <u>interpret</u> as moving from spoken English to Ameslan. <u>Translate</u> means to move from spoken English to manual English, a siglish, or straight fingerspelling, which is rare. <u>Reverse interpret</u> means to move from Ameslan to spoken English, and <u>reverse translate</u> means to move from manual English, a siglish, or fingerspelling into spoken English. Unfortunately, the RID definitions of <u>interpret</u> and <u>translate</u> create more confusion than clarity.

In general, the words <u>interpret</u> and <u>translate</u> refer to two sides of the same coin. <u>To translate</u> usually means moving from one language to another through writing, while <u>interpret</u> refers to an oral rendition of the same act. The key here is that whether interpreting or translating, one is moving from one language to another. According to RID definitions, one <u>interprets</u> only when one goes from English to Ameslan. When one <u>translates</u>, according to the RID, one is not moving from one language to another, but from one medium (oral-aural) to another (visual). It is actually incorrect to call this a translation, for it all occurs in one language, English. A better word for translate, as defined by the RID, would be <u>transliterate</u>. It is analagous to converting English words to Morse Code. The symbols are changed but the language remains the same. The diagram attempts to put into perspective what actually happens.

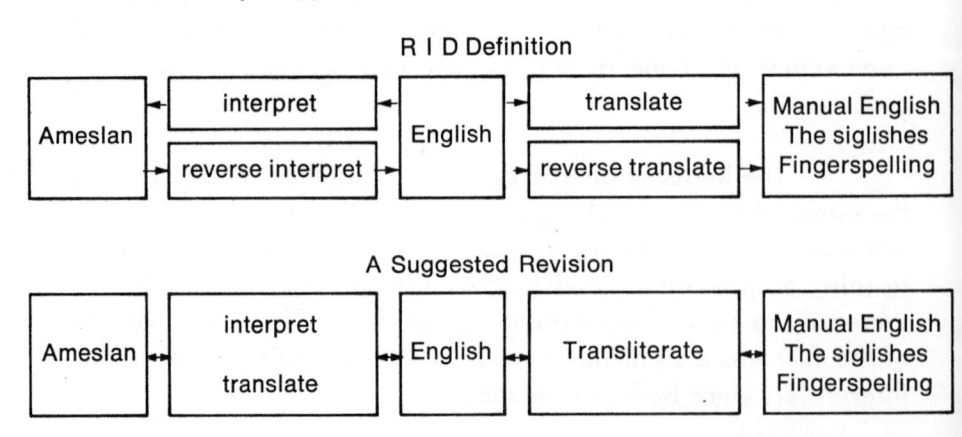

R I D Definition

| Ameslan | ← interpret ← / → reverse interpret → | English | ← translate ← / → reverse translate → | Manual English / The siglishes / Fingerspelling |

A Suggested Revision

| Ameslan | ← interpret / translate → | English | ← Transliterate → | Manual English / The siglishes / Fingerspelling |

Suiting the Action to the Need

During a transliteration, the transliterator can mouth (a voiceless pronunciation of a word) the English while he signs it. The deaf person may read the lips of the transliterator, with the signs complementing the lipreading, or he may concentrate on the signs, using the lipreading to complement the signing. This is, of course, possible only in transliteration. A translation (or interpretation) allows only minimal mouthing. A few words here and there may be mouthed, but it is extremely difficult to do so. Bear in mind that transliteration remains in the same language, whereas

> //Asking an Ameslan translator to mouth English would be somewhat like asking a French-English translator to speak English while writing French.//

translation moves from one language to another. Ameslan has its own structure, which differs greatly from English. Asking an Ameslan translator to mouth English would be somewhat like asking a French-English translator to speak English while writing in French.

Transliteration is used primarily when the deaf person has a good command of English. Usually, he needs to know the exact English words. Generally speaking, this need arises in situations such as classrooms, professional meetings, and discussions of technical subjects. Although the proportion of deaf people who have a good command of English is small, they consume by far the larger share of services offered by interpreters. It is these deaf people who go on to college, attend professional-technical seminars, workshops, and gatherings. Hence, we have the curious situation of having many more competent transliterators than translators.

The need for translators occurs mostly in situations such as court trials, counseling sessions, job interviews, doctors' offices, religious services, and state-association conventions of deaf people.

When the Physician Treats a Deaf Person

The physician should be aware of the disparity among deaf people with respect to their ability to handle English. Thus, he will understand that for certain patients a transliterator is desirable, while for others, a translator is necessary. If neither is available and he must communicate with a deaf patient through writing, he must quickly assess the deaf patient's English fluency and gear his writing to the level of the deaf patient's English comprehension.

If the physician is dealing with a typical deaf person, with or without the services of a translator, he should avoid medical terminology as much as possible. He should speak or write in simple English. He should use as much visual material as possible—for example, anatomy charts, pictures of organs, EKG transcribings, and x-rays. Always remember, the deaf person is visually oriented; he needs to see in order to understand.

Never should a typical deaf person be asked to fill out long, involved, case-history forms. The physician, translator, or receptionist must assist the deaf person in understanding each item and in giving an accurate response.

With regard to selection of a translator-transliterator, the deaf person knows best. He will almost always have a preference for someone he knows. Often, he prefers a family relative. This is understandable, since intimate information is involved. The deaf person, like everyone else, usually feels more comfortable if information is kept within the family circle.

If a translator is used, the physician must take care not to let the translator come between him and his patient. The physician should look at the deaf patient, not toward the translator, while he is speaking. At first, this may feel awkward, because the deaf patient will be looking at the translator most of the time. Nevertheless, a more personal, trusting relationship will ensue if the physician attempts to establish and maintain eye contact.

//Body language, or "body English," is too integral a part of the deaf patient's orientation to be taken idly.//

The physician must ever be conscious of all the nonverbal, visual clues he transmits. The deaf patient places great weight on facial expression, body posture, etc. Body language, or "body English," is too integral a part of the deaf patient's orientation to be taken idly. A pleasant facial expression or a smile may do more to establish the proper physician-patient relationship than anything else.

Rarely should a physician confide to the translator any information he withholds from the patient. If the translator is not a relative, the physician should never convey to him information he does not wish the deaf patient to know. The RID considers this unprofessional, since it involves the translator emotionally, thus impeding his ability to be objective.

In cases of serious or terminal illness, where the physician might withhold information from the patient but release it to the family, he should handle it the same way he would with a hearing patient. He should never discuss anything with the translator—even if the translator is a close friend or member of the family—in the presence of the deaf patient or even if he asks the deaf patient to leave the room. Rather, the physician should telephone the family at a later time and either discuss the situation on the phone or ask a member of the family to come in alone for a consultation. Always observe this axiom: <u>Never say anything in the presence of the deaf patient which you do not wish translated.</u> Very little escapes the deaf person. If he sees the physician talking but the translator not translating, it is only natural that he will become anxious. The deaf person will ask what the physician said, either then or afterward. If the translator refuses to say, he may resent the physician and the translator—and rightly so.

<u>Deaf Children as Patients</u>

When dealing with deaf children, it is advisable to have a parent as the translator or go-between. The physician handles the examination pretty much as he does with hearing children. If the parents are deaf, a translator may be necessary, depending upon their English fluency.

Without question, a deaf patient will consume more of the physician's time than a hearing patient will. Nevertheless, good medical treatment will ensue only if the physician takes the time to establish the necessary rapport. If the deaf patient does not understand the physician or cannot make himself understood, his health may be jeopardized. The extra time spent almost always pays off with an extremely cooperative patient. Furthermore, the physician will experience that rare sense of achievement that comes only when <u>he</u> overcomes the obstacle that deafness places before him.

Ameslan offers promise for an educational breakthrough.

Ameslan: The Communication System of Choice

LOUIE J. FANT, Jr.

IN THE LIGHT OF PERSONAL EXPERIENCE

When I first began teaching deaf children in 1955, a teacher of long experience said to me, "If I did not believe that all deaf children of normal intelligence could master English, I would resign from teaching today." This was a dedicated teacher who had committed his life to finding the path to English fluency for deaf children. I was impressed and sought that same commitment.

Several years later, while teaching at Gallaudet, a famous educator of deaf children said to me, "Louie, you and I have deaf relatives, and we know that most deaf children will never master English." I was shocked to hear this from such an eminent person. I was slightly piqued that, without my permission, he included me as one privy to this knowledge. I was disconsolate that this prestigious man took this pessimistic attitude. If he were correct, I concluded, then the ideal to which I had only a few years prior committed myself was unattainable and thus, a hoax, a mockery. As the first teacher said, I ought to resign, today. So I rejected the pronouncement, arguing that we simply hadn't yet found the way to bring deaf children to English fluency.

Now many years have passed, and I have had a multitude of experiences. This aging process has altered my perspectives and reordered my priorities. Like that well-known educator, I too believe that mastery of English is beyond the reach of most deaf children.

Furthermore, I believe that mastery of English should not dominate first position in our hierarchy of priorities. There are more important considerations. If such is blasphemy against the cherished dogma of our profession, then permit me to attempt to justify it, and make the most of it.

First off, let me say that what I present here are my opinions. I speak as a teacher and observer, not as a scientist. I make no attempt to support my opinions by citing empirically derived facts. Scientific documentation I leave to more capable hands. My opinions are based on my own experiences and the experiences of others.

Education Is More Than Mastery of Subject Matter

Now back to my heresy. I am dismayed by school systems that perceive the task of education as the mastery of a series of subjects. The center of gravity of such systems is not the child, but the subject, the text, the course of study, the syllabus, the lesson plan. It is tooled up to teach content, and takes too little consideration of other values. The system sets the learning and mastery of subject matter as the goal, the end of education itself. The fact is that the mere mastery of subjects is not true education, but rather training. Training children to read, write, cipher, speak, listen, experiment, study, organize, lead, and follow is essential, but does not constitute the goal of true education. A person may do all these things well, yet be poorly educated.

Education takes into account training in skills and subjects, but goes beyond. It is concerned with not only these tangible, concrete phenomena, but also with the intangible, abstract phenomena of human values such as dignity, self-respect, maturity, sophistication, responsibility, security, self-awareness, self-fulfillment, service to others, sensitivity, and creativity. The purpose of training is to help each child realize his full potential as a unique human being, an educated person. The school system that overemphasizes training in skills and subject matter cheats the child of his birthright and heritage.

Why Too Few Deaf Children Become Educated

For years most of us have argued that oralism cheated most deaf children because it
- demanded that all deaf children conform to one system of communication, a system in which only a small number could succeed
- consumed so much time that there was not enough left to teach other essentials
- restricted the pace of learning to the child's progress in oral skills.

The Total Communication movement is freeing us from the shackles of oralism. However, I fear it is replacing oralism with another, equally burdensome yoke: overemphasis on the mastery of English. The Total Communication movement is in danger of repeating the same three errors of oralism:
- insisting that all deaf children communicate only in English, a language in which only a small number will be fluent
- consuming so much time with the teaching of English that there is too little left for other essentials
- restricting the child's progress in learning to his ability to read about and write about a subject in correct English.

The major error of oralism was its undue expenditure of time and energy on an unrealistic task. Will the Total Communication movement slide into this same pit?

The concept ot Total Communication is a rich one, worthy of our noblest sentiments. It embodies the concept of total development of the deaf child. It is an open ended system, not an educational cul de sac. It will thrive only on experimentation, innovation and creativity. It draws substance from diversity, and a plurality of systems. The process of education can be tailored to meet the needs of each child. All this is its promise, but only if it remains total, and does not become restrictive. With regard to communication systems, it must include Ameslan (an acronym for American Sign Language) as well as manual English and other systems.

FIGURE 1   Louie Fant making an Ameslan sign. Depending on the context, he means "to flee in great haste," "to disappear (having fled away)," "to take off," "to cut out," "to split," or "out of sight!'

THE NICETIES OF AMESLAN

The inclusion of Ameslan is far more than a gesture to diversity and plurality. It signifies a recognition of the dignity, the worth, the uniqueness of deaf people. It is an honest act, for it precludes hypocritical attempts to gloss over the fact that deaf people are different from hearing people. It rejects the notion that the more successfully a deaf person can approximate the behavior of hearing people, the worthier a human being he becomes. It says that deaf people should stand tall and proud of what they are, rather than of what they can cleverly imitate. Ameslan insures the deaf child against mere training. It vouches safe his right to an education.

Those who oppose the use of Ameslan in the schoolroom usually do so on the grounds that it impedes the child's development of English. Since Ameslan is easier to handle than manual English, the deaf child will prefer it, thus never discipline himself to learn English. Shades of oralism! Substitute "speech and lipreading" for "English" and "sign language" for "Ameslan" and you hear a much worn record

//Why do we assume that if a child is permitted to follow an easier course, he will never choose a harder one?//

playing a tiresome tune. Why do we assume that if a child is permitted to follow an easier course, he will never choose a harder one? Hans Furth once observed that the logical conclusion of this line of reasoning is that we should forbid children to crawl, else they will never learn to walk, since crawling is easier. Like so many truisms, this one too is a myth. Deaf children should be encouraged to begin with Ameslan. In time, those who can handle it will move into manual English; those who cannot will not be penalized.

Ameslan as a Systematic Subject of Study

When I say that deaf children ought to be encouraged to begin with Ameslan, I am not talking about simply tolerating Ameslan: I am saying that Ameslan should be systematically taught. The children ought to learn to sign it correctly, clearly, and appealingly. They need to have fostered in them a pride in the proper handling of their language. Do we not go to great lengths to teach hearing children the proper handling of English? If a language is not taught in a systematic, codified manner, it degenerates into a plethora of local dialects. This is what has been happening to Ameslan over the last few decades. Graduates of schools for deaf children too often come out signing atrociously because no one has ever taught them to become precise. Indeed, many dismiss it as unimportant. I believe this to be a dangerous trend, dangerous not only to the survival of Ameslan, but also because it may engender in a deaf child a disrespect for English as well. After all, if it doesn't matter how he signs, why should it matter how he writes? I believe pride in Ameslan will motivate most children to strive more diligently to improve their English.

FIGURE 2 This sign means "to be angry or mad," "anger," or "ire."

Pride in Fluency as a Motivating Force

Motivation grows from felt needs, and from interest. If a child, or adult, feels no urgent need to study a subject, or acquire a skill, or he has no interest in doing so, motivating him is an exercise in futility. Unfortunately, most of the skills and knowledge we adults think children must acquire have little appeal to them. So we devise all manner of diversions to trick children into believing they want to do as we wish. Generally, we succeed only in tricking ourselves into believing we have succeeded. If Ameslan were taught as a language, and the children perceived that the adult power structure around them treated their language with respect and dignity, I believe we would see a zest and enthusiasm for learning Ameslan which would transfer to other areas of learning. The deaf child would sense, I think, a need to become skilled in Ameslan. The structure of Ameslan accommodates the requirements of the eye, its logic appeals to the deaf child's perception of the phenomenal world. I

> //If we attempt to explain English to deaf children via Ameslan, I believe we will be rewarded by a more intense effort to learn English.//

believe he would take great pleasure in attending to explanations, discussions of ideas, and sharing experiences in a language he can easily comprehend. Furthermore, if we attempt to explain English to the children via Ameslan, I believe we will be rewarded by a more intense effort to learn English.

Ameslan to Teach English? How?

I do not know whether Ameslan can be used to teach English; to my knowledge, no one has seriously attempted it. It is a curious thing to me that over the past 150 years our profession has shown a remarkable apathy toward this endeavor. We have tried nearly everything else. We have invented the Barry Five Slate System; the Wing Symbols; The Fitzgerald Key; the Croker-Jones Readers; we have enlisted the aid of slide projectors, movie projectors, television, reading machines, teaching machines, computers, and programmed textbooks; we have tried the Oral Method, The Rochester Method, and the Simultaneous Method; and where are we? About where we were 150 years ago, with regard to teaching English. Why don't we apply some money, energy, and brains to exploring how Ameslan might be used to teach English? Isn't it about time for us to exploit this rich resource that has lain dormant on our doorstep all these years?

One answer to these questions is that up until about ten years or so ago, we knew very little about Ameslan as a language. The Annals are thick with articles arguing for the use of sign language or what kinds of signs ought to be used, but no attempts were made, at least to my knowledge, to describe and analyze it as a language. The structure of Ameslan, how it hangs together, is just now being described by linguists around the country. If sufficient money and manpower were focused on describing the structure of Ameslan, we could have a grammar-textbook of the language within one year. With such a book, we could then start experimenting to find ways of teaching English through Ameslan. Furthermore, a book of this kind would serve as a guide for developing other books to teach Ameslan to deaf children, hearing people, and to train teachers (deaf and hearing) of Ameslan classes. A logical, systematically programmed transition from Ameslan to manual English, to written English, can be accomplished only after we thoroughly understand the workings of Ameslan. I believe that an undertaking of this nature would lead to a major breakthrough, the like of which would rank with the foundings of the first schools for deaf children.

REORDERING PRIORITIES—WHAT COMES FIRST

I wrote above that I believe it is unrealistic to expect all, or even most deaf children to master English, and that too high a priority is given to this as a goal. I'd like to elaborate on this. Those who hold the view that the teaching of English is the prime function of our schools generally justify their position by arguing that a deaf person cannot make it in a hearing world without a good command of English. The oralists use the same argument for speech and lipreading, and we know how accurate that is. Certainly, only a fool would maintain that good English, good speech, and good lipreading are not assets. They are desirable, and fortunate is the deaf person who excels in these skills. In terms of helping deaf people make it in a hearing world, however, I think they have been greatly overrated. Any one of us could name scores of deaf people who have lived full, useful, and happy lives with minimal proficiency in these areas. There are other things of equal or greater importance.

Education on the Deaf Child's Territory

It seems to me that what deaf people need most in order to compete in today's market are such things as self-respect, pride, dignity, a sense of worth, confidence, and, perhaps most of all, information and knowledge. These are the fruits of true education. We must cease to concentrate so heavily on the deaf child's liabilities: hearing, speech, and English. We are forever reminding him of his inadequacies, his failure to come up to our standards, by constantly correcting his errors in skills in which he has little chance of succeeding. It is a marvelous wonder that after years of frustration, the deaf child has any will left to keep trying. It shouldn't puzzle us that he has a poor self-image, a crushing sense of inferiority. After all, didn't we tell him so? Neither should we be jolted by his appalling naivete, his lack of sophistication,

> //We should not be jolted by the deaf child's appalling naivete, lack of sophistication, or gauche behavior, since we're the ones who placed a lid on his learning by insisting on immaculate English grammar.//

his gauche behavior, since we're the ones who placed a lid on his learning by insisting on immaculate English grammar. These evils will be removed only when we come to terms with the deaf child on <u>his</u> grounds.

Ameslan can be of tremendous value in correcting many of the things that are wrong about our educational system. The sheer quantity of information, for example, that can be conveyed to and comprehended by the average deaf child via Ameslan, far outdistances that of any other mode. If we had libraries of filmed stories, lectures, and discussions in Ameslan, the deaf child could learn on his own. Courses in deaf studies would aid in developing confidence in his ability. At all age levels, Ameslan and manual English would complement each other, one or the other being used as the child's need and ability warrant and the situation dictates. Only when that happens will we educate the child rather than merely train him.

Deafness shapes unique human beings, with a unique language. We must stop ignoring this uniqueness by our determination to recreate deaf people in the image of hearing people. This world can be a better place to live in simply by helping deaf people make their special contribution to it.

FIGURE 3 Here Louie Fant expresses the words "comical," "funny," or "humorous."

FIGURE 4 The difficult concepts of "who," "whom," or "whose."

Part V:
HEARING CHILDREN OF DEAF PARENTS

Because hearing children of deaf parents communicate via two symbol systems, their language learning ability may be enhanced.

Effects of Parents' Deafness on Hearing Children
●
McCAY VERNON

COMPENSATING FOR LANGUAGE DEFICIENCY: CAN IT BE DONE?

Little research exists on hearing children of deaf parents. Thus, the clinical observations of the author over the last 20 years and the anecodotal views of deaf parents and their children are the primary sources for much of the information that follows.

EFFECTS ON LANGUAGE DEVELOPMENT

Because a profound hearing loss of early onset severely limits language development, deaf parents as a group are severely language deprived. (See Parts III and IV.) In fact some 30 percent of deaf parents are functionally illiterate and only 5 percent reach a tenth-grade academic level (Demographic Studies, 1969; Wrightstone et al, 1962). Reading skills, which are a good measure of receptive language, are at about fourth-grade level.

Sign Language Maintains Communication Level

What these data overlook is that another vernacular—sign language—exists in most of these homes. Bellugi and Klima (1972) suggest that the communication levels achieved by deaf parents with deaf children in sign language approximate those hearing parents attain in spoken English. If this is true, then the children in such families are in a situation analogous to the children of first-generation immigrant parents who may be fluent in their native tongue but restricted in their understanding of English. As a group, children from such homes have no problem mastering English if raised in environments where, with the exception of their parents almost all communication is in English. In the analogy, this is the situation of the deaf child of deaf parents: everyone in his environment speaks English except his parents, who may use sign language exclusively but are far more likely to combine signs with some spoken and fingerspelled English.

Interpreting Sharpens Language Sensitivity

An important, often overlooked point, is that the hearing child of deaf parents often functions as an interpreter for his parents. Interpreting is a demanding skill which greatly sharpens sensitivity for both languages, especially when it is begun very early in life.

When Tradition Goes Unchallenged

Ironically, despite all the data, it has been almost axiomatic for professionals to maintain that hearing children of deaf parents are retarded in language development, yet professionals have had much contact with deaf adults and their children. Most do not know sign language and thus have little basis for their views about hearing children whose mothers and fathers are deaf. The tragedy is that their views have often been taken as fact and deaf parents have been denied adoption rights to hearing children as a result (Feldon, 1966; Nelson, 1966; Villasenor; 1967).

The only research on the topic was by Brelje (1971) who studied 62 deaf children of deaf parents. He found their vocabulary levels to be the same as those of the general population—hearing children of hearing parents. My own clinical observations support Brelje's data. However, the issue is far from resolved. Perhaps the novelist Joanne Greenberg's portrayal of the linguistic difficulties of the daughter of deaf parents from In This Sign is the strongest argument against Brelje's findings.

LOUISA'S STORY

Louisa James was born on an isolated farm in Arkansas at the turn of the century. Both parents were deaf. They communicated with Louisa through a combination of speech and sign language, as do practically all deaf parents. Their articulation was extremely poor in that they omitted many sounds they could not hear or which were hard to imitate from watching the speech of others. Louisa copied this model and spoke with essentially the same articulation patterns as her deaf parents. During infrequent contacts with neighbors and relatives, her speech idiosyncracies were thought to be cute. Thus, they persisted until Louisa entered school.

Louisa's teacher identified her speech problem, and a few months of infrequent speech therapy combined with daily contact with persons who spoke normally corrected the problem. Louisa, in the pattern of Demosthenes, went on to become a speech teacher.

EFFECTS ON SPEECH

The case of Louisa James is an exception that illustrates a rule. Most hearing children of deaf parents do not grow up in isolation from hearing children and adults. Furthermore, in today's times they have television blaring at them almost from the cradle.

Hearing children of deaf parents do not have speech problems, based on my extensive contact with them and on their own views and those of their parents. Brelje's work (1971) is once again the only research available on speech quality. He gave 62 hearing children of deaf parents an articulation test and found their speech to be more intelligible than that of the general population. They may be more articulate because they are more sensitive to the speech process and its related problems as a result of having parents with defective articulation.

ROBIN'S CASE

The Smith parents were both deaf. Their two older children were deaf and in a school for the deaf. The cause for their deafness was genetic. Their third child, Robin, used sign language fluently as a baby and never spoke. At the age of six he enrolled at a school for the deaf where audiological evaluation revealed Robin's hearing was normal. Transferred to a regular first grade, he immediately began to speak normally and progressed satisfactorily in school.

In this case the family and everyone else—including Robin—had just assumed that Robin was deaf because genetic hearing loss pervaded both sides of the family and because the first two children had already been diagnosed as deaf. Robin assumed he was like the rest of the family. Because they did not speak, he did not.

PSYCHOLOGICAL CLIMATE: HEALTHY OR HARMFUL?

The way hearing children cope with their parents' deafness varies from a healthy response to a significant number of pathological reactions, such as hostility, shame, and guilt. In large part the child's reactions are the reflection of the parents' own feelings about their deafness. The parent who accepts his deafness tends to have children who do. In other cases, negative reactions occur when the deaf parents are severely deprived educationally and psychologically. As the hearing children get older they find their parents depending heavily upon them for interpreting, phoning, and basic routines of daily living. They also see the huge gaps in knowledge, the crudeness, and the infantile reactions of adults deprived of education, emotionally healthy childhoods, and basic humanity, by a society insensitive to the needs of deaf people. Children of deaf parents of this type generally reject them and soon start acting out in defiance of parents they are unable to respect.

In marriages where one partner is deaf and the other hearing, the hearing child's reaction to the deaf parent is strongly influenced by the hearing parent's reaction to the deaf spouse. Such marriages are relatively rare.

When Interpretation Is Necessary

An unhealthy tendency noted within some deaf families with a hearing child is that children communicate primarily with the parent who is more oral. This parent or an older child will then function as an interpreter for the other parent, or in the case of the older child, for both parents. This is unhealthy. It reflects the attitudes of hearing family members toward a deaf member. Obviously all children should sign fluently if the parents are deaf. Otherwise communication breaks down.

REFERENCES

Annual Survey of Hearing Impaired Children and Youth: Academic Achievement Test Performance of Hearing Impaired Students in U. S. Washington, DC, Office of Demographic Studies, 1969

Bellugi U, Klima ES: The Roots of Language in the Sign Talk of the Deaf. Psychology Today 6, 61-64, 76, 1972

Brelje HW: A study of the relationship between articulation and vocabulary of hearing impaired parents and their normally hearing children. Unpublished doctoral dissertation. University of Portland, Portland, Oregon, 1971

Feldon D: "Baby Again Ordered Taken from Deaf Couple," Los Angeles Times, San Fernando Valley News, August 2, 1966, 1

Nelson H; "Deaf Couple's Child Raising Ability Questioned," Los Angeles Times, San Fernando Valley News, July 7, 1966, 1

Villasenor R: "Deaf-Mute Couple Win Long Fight for Custody of Boy, Two," Los Angeles Times, San Fernando Valley News, June 2, 1967, 1

Wrightstone JW, Aronow MS, Muskowitz S: Developing Reading Test Norms for Deaf Children, American Annals of the Deaf, 108, 311-316, 1963

Two highly personal accounts of what it's like to grow up in a silent household.

Experiences of Two Hearing Children of Deaf Parents
•
LOUIE J. FANT, JR.
and JOHN S. SCHUCHMAN

LOUIE J. FANT, JR. TELLS HOW HE FELT

It is difficult to be objective about my experience as a hearing child of deaf parents. Undoubtedly I shall overgeneralize from my experience, and for this I apologize. However, that is the obvious point of reference from which to begin.

    I am an only child. My parents and I are very close. They are warm, outgoing, attractive people. I felt, even as an adolescent, that my home life was better than that of most of my friends. That perhaps explains why I was not self-conscious of my parents and never hesitated to invite my hearing friends to my home. My parents made my friends feel comfortable and never embarrassed me. They accomplished this solely by their attitude, for they both lack clear, intelligible speech.

    I learned Ameslan as a child. I cannot recall not knowing it. My parents always communicated with me in Ameslan. Whenever they visited their deaf friends, attended their deaf club, deaf church services, alumni reunions, state-association conventions, and social-recreational events, they always took me with them. I grew up thoroughly familiar with deaf people, their language, and their culture.

My English developed normally because I had relatives nearby. In school, reading and spelling were my best subjects. I did have a slight deficiency in vocabulary, but that was made up by the time I reached the third grade. I recall missing only one thing: sound. When I got my first radio I ran it day and night, just to have sound in the house.

My parents rarely asked me to be their interpreter. I am grateful they didn't ask. I would discourage deaf parents from using their hearing children too frequently as interpreters for anything other than phone calls and neighborhood small talk. For important transactions, an adult interpreter should be called in. I feel interpreting

> //Interpreting places a great deal of pressure on a child. He is required to understand adult language and translate it into appropriate Ameslan, and he will likely be too immature to do this.//

places a great deal of pressure on a child. He is required to understand adult language and translate it into appropriate Ameslan, and he will likely be too immature to do this. Furthermore, the child may resent being placed in this uncomfortable position.

I had no concept of why my parents wrote poor English until I entered graduate school. It seems incredible to me that I had not grasped the connection between their English and their deafness, but such was the case. I suspect the same is true of many hearing children of deaf parents.

Thus, when they are forced into interpreting situations, they may become embarrassed by their parents' English, being ignorant of the cause.

I knew hearing children who were extremely defensive about their deaf parents. Other hearing children taunted them about their parents. In all the cases I knew personally, a happy, strong relationship did not exist between parents and child. I have no other explanation for the fact that this was not the case with me. My parents made me feel secure. I suppose that is another way of saying that there are good and bad deaf parents, just as is the case with hearing people.

Many benefits accrued to me because of my parents' deafness. Their move from a small southern town to a large metropolitan southwestern city during World War II occurred as a result of their wish to work in an airplane factory which hired large numbers of deaf people. The move brought me into contact with a much larger world than I would have known otherwise.

In our new home, my parents attended a large, wealthy church which had services for deaf people. The middle-and upper-class virtues of the church became a part of my ethic. I was able to attend college on a scholarship provided by this church.

Finally, a career of working with deaf people undoubtedly directly resulted from my lifelong association with them. My life and career have been enriched and exciting because my parents are deaf. It seems sad and tragic that all hearing children of deaf parents have not had a similar experience.

JOHN S. SCHUCHMAN'S EXPERIENCE

Since I did not maintain a written record of my childhood,

this account is subjective. I am an only child, a hearing child of low-verbal deaf parents who communicated via what is now called Ameslan. My parents were painfully aware of their inadequate formal education, and as a result, they made every effort to insure that I was surrounded by books. My parents took me to the library on a regular basis and they were prey to a host of book and encyclopedia salesmen. In addition, both of my parents read a great deal themselves, mostly newspapers and popular magazines.

//It is ironic that the only deaf child I knew was the child of hearing parents. He spent many of his nonschool hours at our home simply because we could communicate with him.//

My parents' friends were non-Gallaudet College deaf people. It is ironic that the only deaf child I knew (other than those times we visited the school for the deaf class reunions) was the child of hearing parents. His name was Gilbert and he spent many of his nonschool hours at our home simply because we could communicate with him. In addition, all of my hearing cousins and neighborhood friends could at least fingerspell so he had a readymade peer group near his home. Since deaf people do not live in deaf ghettos, we would often visit my parents' deaf friends, all of whom had hearing children. Again, all of these children communicated in Ameslan to varying degrees. To the best of my knowledge, I was the only child among the children of my parents' deaf friends who went to college. I believe this was a function of socioeconomic factors (all of my parents' friends were blue-collar workers) and not deafness per se. My personal motivation for college was the fact that I was very much impressed by a Boy Scout leader whom I knew to be a college graduate. I now have a Ph.D. in history and a law degree.

As I look back, two things were very painful to me as a hearing child of deaf parents. (I might add that I had the usual fights when my peers would occasionally mock my parents, but I view that as no different from the same kind of problem faced by children of immigrant parents.) First, I was the interpreter for my family, primarily at my mother's insistence. My father was much more independent. I interpreted everything from loan negotiations to simple grocery transactions, and I did this at a very young age. At the time, it was very painful, but I now realize that it taught me patience and diplomacy (for example, I did not always interpret what my parent was really saying about the insurance salesman). Most of all, it taught me a sense of responsibility and gave me an ability to do things that I did not particularly enjoy doing, a talent very useful in later life. Second, my mother, who loved me very much and who took great pride in my accomplishments, used to accuse me of being ashamed of my parents' deafness whenever I balked at doing something desired of me. Although I am not a psychologist, I suspect that most hearing children experience such emotions; indeed, I would think it strange if they did not. In my case, it was a whip used against me. If I can be permitted any advice to deaf parents of hearing children, I would recommend that they never accuse their children of being ashamed of their parents, even when they suspect it is true. An understanding parent can handle that problem in other ways.

In sum, my parents gave me their love and support. My mother is deceased but my father now lives with my wife and me. He and I remain very close to each other today. I am convinced that my experience as a hearing child of deaf parents made me a better person than I might have otherwise been. Needless to say, it is impossible to generalize from my experience to that of others. It is interesting to note that most of the literature concerns itself with deaf children of hearing and deaf parents; it is too bad that we hearing children did not anticipate this and maintain anecdotal records of our experiences.

Index
KIETH C. WRIGHT

Alport's disease, 40
American School for the Deaf, 105
American Sign Language, 189
Ameslan, 172, 190, 195, 208, 209; conceptual framework, 196; nonverbal aspects, 197; role in teaching English, 211
Audiometry: behavioral, 48; differential diagnosis, 20; impedence, 26, 38, 48; infants, 48
Auditory-evoked potentials, 48, 49
Auditory meatus, 39
Auditory training in habilitation, 48
Cerebellopontile angle tumors, 29-31
Childhood behavior disorder, 70-71
Child's adjustment to deafness, 3, 10, 66
Chronic mastoid disease, 39
Combined method of communication, 139, 195
Communication: Ameslan, 172, 190, 195, 208; combined method, 139, 195; controversy, 4, 109, 168; cued speech, 195; oral method, 110, 138; reverse interpreting, 200; Rochester method, 110, 140, 194; Seeing Essential English, 193; Signing Exact English (SEE), 111, 193; sign language, 15, 48, 79, 111, 175, 189; simultaneous communication, 5, 110, 139, 194; speech- and lip-reading, 6; Total Communication, 5, 111, 113, 144, 146, 147, 179, 182, 197, 198, 207, 208; Visual English, 111, 193
Comparative development of deaf and hearing children, 63
Congenital rubella, diagnosis, 37
Consanguinity of parents, 34
Day schools, 108
Deaf adolescents, parents' reaction to, 68
Deaf adults: frequency of psychosis, 68; role in educating deaf children, 165
Deaf children: behavior disorders, 71; of deaf parents, 76, 158; education, 11, 136, 163-168, 207, 213; functional illiteracy, 96; isolation, 97; language acquisition, 4; language

development, 221-222;
predictions, 42; psychological
development, 55; psychosis, 69;
reading level, 67; research, 166;
teaching methods, 125-126
Deaf education, 132
Deafness: acquired, 20; as an
adaptive limitation, 61; and
autism, 45; causes, 21, 29;
definition, 89; diagnosis delay, 89;
effect on language development,
220; etiology, 41; genetic, 20, 43;
misdiagnosis, 90; and neuroses, 68;
and organic diseases, 69;
prediction, 42, 43; unknown
origin, 20
Deaf schools, 139
Deaf teachers, 126
Denial of deafness, 73
Differential diagnostic problems, 90
Disabilities: coping mechanisms, 92;
denial among professionals, 94;
psychological denial, 93
Early childhood, 36
Education, 101-188; of parents, 2
Electronystagmographic analysis, 39
Family histories, diagnostic
importance of, 20
Family trees in clinical
diagnosis, 35
Fingerspelling, 190
Funduscopic eye examination, 37
Gallaudet College, 106
Gallaudet, TH, 104
Genetic counseling, 43
Genetic history, 36
Genetic hypotheses about
deafness, 42
Habilitative resources, 48, 51,
52, 80
Hearing aids, 23, 48, 112
Hearing: and Communication, 104;
and learning, 103
Hearing children of deaf parents,
223-225
Hearing impaired, 36, 135
Hearing loss: definition, 135;
family history, 35; residual, 112;
role in development, 78

Heterochromia, 38
Intellectual development, 59
Intelligence tests, 151, 154
Interpret, definition, 200
Interpreters, 199, 203
Language: in child development,
62; communication, 79, 107;
conveyer of emotion, 63
Language development, 58, 62, 66
Leiter intelligence scale, 155
Manual communication, 138, 181;
development, 116; early
childhood, 115; new status, 167;
parental reaction, 73
Manual English, 111, 190
Marriages among the deaf, 144
Mastoid x-rays, 39
Medical care, 2, 21
Medical history, 35
Mentally retarded children and
hearing evaluation, 47
Mental retardation, 46
Middle ear: abnormalities in
otitis media, 25; examinations,
23; normal anatomy, 24
Minimal brain dysfunction, 70
Motor retardation, 39
Multiply handicapped deaf
children, 69, 90
Nasopharyngoscopic examinations, 38
Neurosensory hearing loss, 23, 31-41
Noise trauma, 36
Only hearing ear, 30
Oral communication, 110, 138
Oral education of the deaf, 105
Oral schools, 139
Otalgia, 31, 32
Otitis externa, 27-28
Otitis media, 22, 23, 27
Otological care of the deaf child, 22
Otorrhea, 32, 33
Ototoxicity, 36
Parent-child communication, 3, 13,
67, 79
Parents' reactions, 2, 3, 10, 64, 66,
75, 87, 89, 95, 97
Physician: patient relations, 202;
reaction to deafness, 1; role in
care of deaf patient, 50

Postlingual deafness, 134
Prelingual deafness, 134, 166
Progressive hearing loss, 50
Renal disease, 40
Receptive language, 118
Registry of Interpreters for the Deaf (RID), 199
Residential schools, 106-109
Resources for help, 7
Reverse interpreting, 200
Rochester method, 110, 140, 194
Rubella, 39
Seeing Essential English, 111, 193
Self-differentiation in infancy, 56
Siglish, 191
Signed English, 111, 193
Sign language, 15, 48, 79, 111, 119, 122, 123, 175, 189
Signs, 119, 122, 123
Simultaneous communication, 5, 110, 139, 194

Smiling response, 56
Speech development, 67
Speech- and lip-reading, 6, 22, 96, 110
Thinking and verbal language, 63
Thyroid abnormalities, 38
Tinnitus, 32, 33
Total Communication, 5, 111, 113, 144, 146, 147, 179, 182, 197, 198, 207, 208
Transient hearing loss, 36
Traumatic perilymphatic fistula, 31
Treponema pallidium immobilization, 40
Tympanic membrane examination, 23
Tympanometry, 26
Vestibular function tests, 29
Visual English, 111, 193
Waardenburg's disease, 38
Waldenstrom's macroglobulinemia, 40